Bird of Paradox

The Seasoning of
Birdie McInnes

J.C. Mitchell

LUMINARE PRESS
WWW.LUMINAREPRESS.COM

AUTHOR'S NOTE

This book describes the author's experiences growing up Catholic in Portland, Oregon, during the 1950s, 1960s, and 1970s and reflects his opinions relating to those experiences.

Names, descriptions, and details of individuals identified in this book have been changed to protect their privacy. Any resemblance to other people, events, places, or situations is strictly coincidental.

With the exception of brief quotes from songs and scholarly articles, no part of this book may be stored, copied, or reproduced in any manner without written permission of the author, agent, publisher, or legally recognized copyright holder.

Bird of Paradox: The Seasoning of Birdie McInnes
Copyright © 2021 by J.C. Mitchell

All rights reserved. This book or any portion thereof may not be reproduced or used in any manner whatsoever without the express written permission of the publisher, except for the use of brief quotations in a book review.

Printed in the United States of America

Luminare Press
442 Charnelton St.
Eugene, OR 97401
www.luminarepress.com

LCCN: 2021913865
ISBN: 978-1-64388-707-4

For Jacy Carmen, Carlotta Nitta, and Gemma Emilia with all my love

Contents

Acknowledgments ... ix

Prologue ... 1

1. The Luck of the Draw ... 5
2. Descent into Darkness ... 31
3. Fleeing the Maelstrom ... 56
4. Manic Migration ... 66
5. New Day Dawning ... 78
6. Mobilizing a Transition ... 85
7. Dream Season ... 93
8. Welcome to Eugene ... 119

Acknowledgments

Countless individuals—whether they know it or not—contributed to this book. It would be easy to suggest that I have spent most of my life writing it, though I may not have always been aware of that fact. As Ernest Hemingway noted, "In order to write about life, you must live it."

Within the pages of this book, many of the people who contributed to its existence were teachers. Teaching is, indeed, the greatest profession, or as Aristotle noted, "Teaching is the highest form of understanding."

What follows are special acknowledgments of teachers who have made a difference in my life, particularly when it comes to the art of writing and communication.

First and foremost, I must recognize Sister Maria, Order of St. Francis, my eighth grade teacher at the Catholic elementary school I attended. She was a special kind of teacher: smart, caring, inspirational, and empathetic. It would be no exaggeration to note that she turned my life around at a most critical period. Years later, she left the order and resumed her life as Margie Rojas Lensch, teaching for many years in the Los Angeles School District.

When it comes to recognizing those who encouraged me as a writer and trained me in the art of communication, I need look no further than the University of Oregon

School of Journalism, where my mentors included Ken Metzler, Dean Rea, Duncan McDonald, Roy Paul Nelson, Roy Halverson, and many others. I also thank Dick and Polly Keusink, my editors when I worked at the *Brookings-Harbor Pilot* in Brookings, Oregon.

Many thanks to Jenn Casey, Tom Maloney, and Mark Kirchmeier for assistance in editing and Melissa Hart for editorial and publication guidance. Major kudos to Kathy Kifer, graphic designer/illustrator extraordinaire, for the book cover.

I'd be remiss if I didn't note a special tribute to my grandmother and my parents as having played vital roles in my education and upbringing. I could not have reached my goals or accomplished much of anything without their critical assistance, and for that I am eternally grateful.

Finally, thanks to my family: Rebecca, Gina, and Jory, who watched me write, edit, rewrite, edit, and write some more on this book.

J.C.M.

Prologue

"The world is a contradiction; the universe, a paradox."

—Kedar Joshi, Indian mathematician

Robert Cameron McInnes was like every other kid growing up Catholic in fifties and sixties America, yet in many ways, he was unique. The nuns called him Bert, but everyone else knew him as Birdie. The eldest child of five, Birdie attended grammar school at Our Lady of Perpetual Sorrow (OLPS) parish, like all the other Italian American and Irish American youth in his neighborhood. "Parish" was an all-inclusive term that meant the priests, nuns, clerics, congregation, school, and staff.

These young Christian soldiers were, by and large, serious about their schooling, and many were actively involved in other traditions and rituals of the Roman Catholic Church. Some, like Birdie, were altar boys—those young servers who assisted the priest in conducting Mass while attaining a certain degree of proficiency in the lost language of Latin. At OLPS, Birdie experienced his first taste of the type of draconian discipline the Catholics administered. Brother Gerard, the parish advisor for the Altar Boy Society, like other members of the Franciscan order, subscribed to the twin Catholic concepts of distributing guilt and—when necessary—corporal punishment.

The altar boys were an ambitious lot. Many were also members of the Boy Scouts of America, which was in its heyday at the time. Many played sports, and some, like Birdie, had newspaper delivery routes as well. In addition to serving Mass at the parish church every morning, they assisted the parish priests by serving Mass at an earlier service at a monastery nearby at the ungodly hour of 6:00 a.m. Sometimes it seemed only the cloistered nuns, who were basically imprisoned at the monastery, and a few devout senior citizens were in attendance.

One morning, Birdie overslept, and having to choose between serving Mass and delivering the morning edition of *The Oregonian*, he chose the latter. *It'll be okay*, he reasoned uncomfortably, assuming the other server would pick up the slack. Big mistake. At the next meeting of the OLPS Altar Boy Society, retribution would be swift and brutal.

"McInnes, stand and follow me," barked Brother Gerard at the beginning of the meeting.

Birdie's heart leapt into his throat. What followed was the most serious upbraiding Birdie had yet received from an adult in a position of authority, at least up to that point in his life. Brother Gerard had him in tears for the serious offense of missing the early Mass, and altar boys on the other side of the door could hear every word. When it was over, Birdie asked Brother Gerard if he could at least clean up a bit before facing the others. "No," growled the sadistic cleric firmly. "Get back in there and sit down."

Birdie returned to his seat, eyes red and swollen and his ego shattered more by humiliation in front of his peers than anything Brother Gerard had said. The stout, muscular cleric had accomplished two tasks at once: disciplined an errant altar boy and sent a clear message to all others in the room who might be so careless as to miss a scheduled Mass: "Don't even think about it."

It wouldn't be the last time Birdie experienced swift and brutal Catholic justice. They didn't refer to these clerics as "soldiers of Christ" for nothing. The altar boys, at least the errant ones, would nonetheless have their payback behind the scenes, munching on communion hosts and sipping cheap Thunderbird wine surreptitiously in the sacristy after hours.

CHAPTER ONE

The Luck of the Draw

Winter 1972: The big day would be a Thursday, just like all other significant days in the life of Robert Cameron McInnes. On this day, along with all the American young men born in 1952, Birdie would learn his draft number. Plan A was to receive a high draft number. The Vietnam War was limping along, but despite increasing outcry by the national media and the general populace, young Americans were still being drafted into the military. What if he received a low draft number? What then?

Most unfortunately for Birdie, many of the old excuses for avoiding military service during the Vietnam War had evaporated like a summer rainstorm in the Alvord Desert. College deferment? Revoked the year before. Bad back or flat feet? Not likely, considering that Birdie played linebacker and backup quarterback on the high school football team. Conscientious objector status? An unseemly task with little chance for success. Marriage deferment? Possible, except for one significant issue: a woman. Who would he talk into marriage? Perhaps he could convince his erstwhile girlfriend, Sally Bauer.

However, the issue could be a moot point if he scored a high-enough number in the lottery. It was not that Birdie was incapable of serving in the US military. He simply had no interest, though he dared not share that feeling with his father, a former marine officer. Birdie's cousin, Jimbo Parker, had served in Vietnam, and after stepping on a land mine, what was left of him was shipped back to the United States in a box. He had succumbed to his injuries while on patrol during the Tet Offensive in 1968.

Apprehensive about the prospect of fighting what he considered a useless war in Southeast Asia, Birdie had no interest in dying. He knew he would qualify. Unfortunately, he also had a penchant for finding trouble and knew inherently the military would not be a good fit. That day, Birdie and Sally sat by the radio—the lottery was too insignificant to broadcast on television. When the count reached 50, Birdie thought, *Okay, so far, so good.* Then the hammer dropped. Birdie's number—based on his birthday in 1952—came up at 56. For Birdie, Plan A was no longer an option, so it was time to examine Plans B, C, and D.

Growing up in Portland, Oregon, in the late 1950s was as idyllic an experience as could be found anyplace else in America. For the first time in two generations, neither war nor economic disaster occupied America's sensibilities. Racial strife, still a serious undercurrent, wouldn't boil over until the sixties. Communism in Russia, China, and other—mostly Third World—countries had just become a serious threat to the American way of life. America had a grandpa in the White House: Dwight D. Eisenhower, commander of the Allied forces in Europe during World War II and a national hero.

Life was good, but Birdie knew from an early age that life was also a paradox. After struggling at birth as a premature infant, and weathering a bout of pneumonia at the age of two months, he blossomed due to the nurturing approach of his mother and grandmother. Birdie grew up in a matriarchy because his dad was off in the hinterlands of Oregon, attempting to establish a career as a science teacher. Living with his gramma and mom was a blissful experience: good food, good company, and good times. When his brother, Emile, was born, he was gifted a playmate and lifelong friend, but their lives were about to change radically.

In 1957, reality bit Birdie and Emile squarely on the buttocks when their father moved back to Portland to stay. He had been off working on remote teaching assignments in various and sundry locations, trying to establish himself, moving from small Oregon villages from Ukiah to Powers to Sutherlin to Forest Grove and finally to Vancouver, Washington, just across the Columbia River from the City of Roses. At that point, the family reunited with their dad, who had purchased a home in East Portland. Life for the McInnes siblings would henceforth change drastically.

Birdie's mom told the boys that his dad had never wanted children or even to get married for that matter. No one knew exactly why she said that, though his true nature was obvious through the elder McInnes's gruff demeanor and constant mood swings. While the McInnes lads lived at their gramma's house for the first half decade of their lives, their dad came home only once or twice a year. When he was a year old, Emile, puzzled and frightened by the presence of a stranger in their home, didn't recognize his own father. Mom said their dad could inexplicably become an "old goat," but that description was misleading. Around others, he could be charming, even patronizing to an extent, with his friends and acquaintances. He wanted people to like and respect him. Family, however, was a different matter. Birdie and his siblings weren't sure what to make of his attitude, but they had their suspicions and theories.

For one thing, their dad was a classic narcissist. Plus, he suffered from an obsessive need to please his own father, their grandfather, for whatever reason. Birdie and Emile believed that he likely suffered a serious guilt complex that he never could shake because of his behaviors and misdeeds during his youth that had caused alienation from his parents and siblings. Birdie and Emile, as two among many raised Catholic, had so much guilt drilled into their heads by the nuns and priests at OLPS that they developed an immunity. Those students unable to shake the guilt ultimately succumbed to personality disorders for the rest of their lives. Their dad could be nice when he wanted to be, but he was mostly impatient, insulting, and even violent. Something deep down inside of him clearly affected him, but nobody knew exactly what, though there were indications from others. His own parents and siblings, for example, didn't like him and even avoided him whenever they could.

Portland was off the beaten path if you were from the East Coast, but make no mistake; the City of Roses was no small town. At nearly four hundred thousand inhabitants, it was the thirty-third-largest city in the United States. Birdie grew up in East Portland. The suburbs were starting to boom. Home building grew exponentially, and a new concept in American consumerism—shopping malls—was in its infancy. Birdie, the older of two children (so far), started school in 1958 at OLPS. His dad, Cyril William McInnes, was a Canadian American of Scottish and Irish heritage whose parents were from Halifax, Nova Scotia. His mom—Anna Maria Bricchetto—was the daughter of Italians from Genoa who immigrated to Portland. In terms of personality, Birdie was, generally speaking, polite and somewhat reserved in public. He had been well trained by his gramma. Only later would his heritage prove to be a lethal cocktail.

Birdie, Emile, and their mom left Gramma's house for a new life with Dad. The family purchased its first television, a black-and-white Zenith, in 1957. Soon, the two boys were joined by three more siblings: Douglas James, Carlotta Anna, and Stevie Jo. Birdie and Emile whiled away the hours after school watching action-adventure shows like *The Lone Ranger*, based on stories by Zane Grey, and *Superman*, based on the Action Comics superhero. Disney and Warner Brothers cartoons were also popular: Mickey Mouse, Donald Duck, Goofy (a strangely befuddled dog-person), Pluto (a real dog in caricature), Bugs Bunny, Porky Pig, and Daffy Duck (Birdie's favorite character, who had lines like "suffering succotash" and "I'm a traveling salesman from Walla Walla, Washington") were all staples on the odd new tube.

Television would swiftly replace radio as the medium of choice in America. Live action comedies featured *The Three Stooges* and *Abbott and Costello*. Quiz shows like *What's My Line* and *Name That Tune* were popular among adults, as were *The Jack Benny Show* and *The Red Skelton Show*. Both of the latter entertainers were originally vaudevillians who had made the transition to radio and now television. *The Lawrence Welk Show* was also popular among adults of all ages. Welk was the "oompa-oompa" band conductor famous for his line, "a-one and a-two…" Birdie's gramma adored Lawrence Welk, and Birdie was obliged to watch The Lennon Sisters and accordionist Myron Floren.

Birdie especially enjoyed mystery and horror television shows like *The Twilight Zone* and *Alfred Hitchcock Presents*. Hitchcock opened his show with a dark and foreboding "good evening." In Birdie's favorite episode of *The Twilight Zone*, the protagonist had somehow discovered a stopwatch that could halt time: when he clicked the button on the top of the watch, people froze in their tracks as if they had turned into pillars of salt. The character had a lot of fun robbing donut stores and banks until he dropped the watch, shattering the bewitched timepiece. The show ended with the protagonist grimly pondering the prospect of a lonely future lost among millions of human mannequins frozen in time.

The new medium also featured commercial advertisements during shows, known popularly as "commercials." These interruptions, commonly known as ads (unbeknown to Birdie at the time) paid for programming and, of course, the salaries of executives, producers, actors, and stunt doubles along with the staff and equipment needed to support the burgeoning industry.

Birdie lived not too far from a local market where bubble gum and other candies were available for a mere penny apiece. Naturally, he spent a lot of time at the store reading comic books and purchasing his favorite bubble gum, Bazooka Joe. Characterized on the wrapper as a bizarre-looking fellow with a turtleneck sweater, Joe had blond, spiky hair. Once opened, the gum wrapper had a three-frame cartoon inside. Birdie could stuff ten pieces of gum in his mouth at once, and tiring his jaw while chewing, he would promptly forget to read the three-frame cartoons.

The store, Hughes Market, featured a magazine rack with a reading area for those folks who were unable—or perhaps unwilling—to purchase the slick, glossy journals. For kids, the rack featured magazines like *Jack and Jill* and, of course, comic books illustrating the adventures of superheroes like Superman, Batman, Captain America, and Iron Man. For teenagers, the store stocked Archie and Jughead comics and other teen magazines featuring humorous storylines of young love. For adults, magazines on display were *Time*, *Look*, *Life*, and *Photoplay*. While the former three were general-interest publications outlining national and world news, the latter extolled the likes of Marlon Brando, Tony Curtis, and other "movie stars" in the halcyon days of Hollywood.

One day, Birdie noticed a new magazine on the rack titled *Playboy*. Curious, he picked up a copy, and because he had yet to learn how to read well other than "See Dick run. See Jane run," he gazed at the pictures, which featured half-naked young women in fetchingly sultry poses. Despite the fact that he was some half dozen years away from puberty, he found the pictures strangely compelling. He was intrigued to the point that, going against form for him, he slipped the picture book under his shirt. Walking out the door with the contraband under his shirt, he felt a large, hairy hand on his shoulder. "Son, come with me," said the burly proprietor.

Birdie wasn't exactly sure about what kind of trouble he was in. Just a six-year-old, he thought he might receive a stern lecture by the store manager. Unfortunately, his luck had run out. He was unaware of the concept of two-way mirrors and was caught red-handed stealing the *Playboy* magazine from Hughes Market. The gruff, bald-pated proprietor gave him the third degree, extracting his parents' phone number. Soon he was ushered home by his parents; both were sullen and quiet.

What was going through their heads? In hindsight, what could they have been thinking about a six-year-old stealing possibly the only thing in the market that could be considered pornography? His mom was probably thinking, *Hopefully the lad's father will only beat him until he can't walk when we get home and not kill him outright.* His dad was probably thinking, *Thank God the boy isn't a homosexual.* Likely, they were both incredulous. Neither spoke on the way home from Hughes Market. The subject appeared to be closed, because Birdie was neither beaten nor verbally abused. Unknowingly, he had experienced his first taste of empathy.

Plan A (a high draft lottery number) ultimately led to Plans B, C, and D. In Birdie's mind, it was always good to have a backup strategy. If Plan A didn't pan out, he thought Plan B would be to apply for conscientious objector status. After all, he was a good Catholic boy for the most part. His high school buddy, Mike Donahue, was in the same boat: they were both born on the same day in 1952.

All their friends, it seemed, had numbers ranging from 250–365. In other words, most had good reason to assume they were safe, yet Birdie and Mike did not know where they stood in terms of draft status. That changed after Birdie received a notice from his local draft board and was ordered to report for a pre-induction physical.

On the appointed day, Birdie reported to the Armed Forces Entrance Examination Service (AFEES) center in downtown Portland with all the other unlucky shmucks with low lottery numbers. The AFEES center, a dark and foreboding facility, resembled a meat-processing plant. The group received a series of tests to determine their suitability for military service.

Their first assignment was to line up and strip naked for an anal cavity search. Why they wanted to examine his asshole was lost upon Birdie. This humiliating experience was followed by a series of tests to check eyesight, hearing, and other physical features. Naturally, he had to pee into a bottle for a drug test. The examination took approximately six hours. At the end of the day, he was relieved to get the hell out of that place.

On the way out, he queried the attendant at the front desk, "Do you have any idea how high the numbers will go this year in terms of the draft?"

"Well, son, I'd guess they'll probably take up to about 125 or so this year," he said matter-of-factly.

Birdie knew full well that the Vietnam War was winding down. Troop numbers in Southeast Asia, which had peaked at about five hundred thousand in 1969, were diminishing following the Tet Offensive, the brutal assault Vietcong and North Vietnamese troops conducted to break the will of the American forces. Many US soldiers died in that battle, and the American people—particularly young people and those who had lost their sons fighting the communists in a far-off land—were growing uneasy.

War protests mounted; Birdie himself participated in several "war moratorium" rallies in downtown Portland in conjunction with similar events around the United States. The increasing disenchantment with the war had already led to the demise of one US president—Lyndon Baines Johnson from Texas—and the new leader, Richard Nixon from California, elected in 1968, was on the hot seat to end the war—and fast.

Nixon's new policy of "Vietnamization" was slowly starting to reduce the number of troops in Southeast Asia (the term was more accurate than Vietnam, because the United States was fighting in the neighboring countries of Laos and Cambodia). The military, as characterized by General Curtis LeMay, wanted to "bomb (the enemy) back to the Stone Age." That wasn't fast enough for most people in this country who wanted the war ended immediately.

Faced with the fact that he would be drafted, Birdie reluctantly turned to Plan B: filling out the necessary paperwork for what could only be described as a tribunal. A board of three officials would determine his qualifications for conscientious objector (CO) status. Two weeks later, on Leap Year Day—February 29, 1972—Birdie had his day in court. The tribunal consisted of two men and a woman representing the local draft board. All three sat on one side of a rectangular table and appeared stern and conservative. None were smiling or engaging. Birdie sat on the opposite side of the table, facing his humorless inquisitors.

"Why are you applying for conscientious status?" asked the woman abruptly as she tapped her pencil on the table.

"Well," Birdie answered solemnly, "I'm a lifelong Catholic who subscribes to the concept of peace on earth as preached by Jesus…"

She cut him off. "Well, young man, according to your school records and police blotter, you were suspended by your high school six times for fighting and have been arrested as a minor in possession of alcohol on a number of occasions. How do you respond to that?"

Uh-oh, he thought. *These people have done their homework. How could I be so naïve as to think they would ask a few questions, call it good, and send me on my way?* Sitting there dumbfounded, he didn't have an answer.

"Request denied," she said with an emotionless and unsympathetic glaze. The men nodded solemnly.

Son of a bitch, Birdie thought. *I've been knocked out two minutes into the first round.* It was on to Plan C.

Birdie met his lifelong running mates—Peter Thomas Talbot, Timothy Luis Moriarity, and his brother, Neil, among others—in the classrooms and schoolyard of OLPS in 1959. Birdie, P.T., and Lu', as they were known, formed an unholy trinity for authorities of all stripes over the next fifteen years. Their meeting was a sign of things to come.

Birdie's church and school near Mt. Tabor

One day during recess, Birdie and a few other classmates were having a difficult exchange with the schoolyard bully: George Fink, a large fellow with an attitude. Fed up with Fink's taunting and bullying, Birdie approached Lu' about a plan of action.

"I have an idea," said Lu'. "Let's get P.T. over here."

P.T. was undersized but muscular and quick, both with his fists and his temper. After quick introductions, P.T. asked about the issue at hand.

"Well," Birdie said, "we want you to beat the crap out of George Fink."

Not even waiting for an explanation, P.T. walked across the schoolyard and coldcocked the much larger Fink, knocking him to the asphalt with a bloody nose. The ensuing hubbub abruptly ended recess when the nuns intervened.

Over the course of time, the cadre of Birdie, Lu', Neil, and P.T. formed a powerful lightning rod for trouble. Despite their relatively respectable resumes as altar boys, Boy Scouts, and student athletes, "the boys," as they liked to call themselves, could be the scourge of the neighborhood, feared by public school kids and loathed by parents with daughters. Despite their reputations as hooligans, the boys all knew how to work a room. The chemistry of the classroom would change when the boys, talented, bright and articulate, were in the house. Classmates felt their presence when they entered a room. In a time when kids were to be seen and not heard, the boys even struck grown-ups mute with their powerful personalities.

These lads made unique foils for the OLPS nuns, whom they viewed as fascists in habits. The nuns ran the grammar school, a grade 1–8 facility, with iron wills. Though they came in various shapes, sizes, and ages, all were college educated, and some had advanced degrees, having majored in such fields as theology or counseling psychology. The school had an even distribution of nuns and lay teachers, but the nuns ran the show. Despite their outward appearance of piety, one and all could be mean, some more than others. And scary. The nuns could be intimidating to a youngster.

Most of the time, their scary nature was intentional. Occasionally, their manner was incidental, like on November 22, 1963, when the Mother Superior, Sister Elizabeth, blurted frantically over the public address system, "The president has been shot!" The riveting announcement that President John F. Kennedy had been shot by an assassin named Lee Harvey Oswald would make for a vivid memory for those in attendance. The boys had issues with authority, but what made them the scourge of the nuns likewise made them folk heroes to some classmates. Plus, they were funny without having to tell jokes, smart without having to recite church doctrine, and popular without pretentiousness. They were formidable opponents, but so were the nuns. The conflict created an interesting dynamic.

This antagonism between the boys and the nuns continued throughout the sixties. More chess match than life on a chain gang, the back and forth put the Franciscan nuns at OLPS on the horns of a dilemma: the boys were sharp, and they had magnetism and charisma. Generally a big pain in the ass, they were creative and even fearless in the many escapades they devised. Whether peeing in the drinking fountains or sending some unsuspecting geek into the girls' restroom to examine the "comb machine" (a Kotex dispensary), taping firecrackers to school windows on Halloween, or stealing the carpets in the church vestibule, the boys made life interesting for the nuns. All enigmas, they were incapable of avoiding trouble, but they were especially intelligent, charming, and inexplicably self-assured.

P.T., the oldest of the trio though just by months, was the third of four children. His dad had passed away in an industrial accident when he was young. His mom remarried a widower with two kids of his own, creating a Brady Bunch kind of family that blended well. Lu' was number ten in a family of thirteen children. Birdie was the oldest in a family of five, normal for a Catholic family in the sixties when family size averaged two adults for every six kids. How could any parent even attempt to keep track of all those kids? They couldn't, and as a result, the boys were more or less freelancers left to their own devices. They took full advantage. They could be cruel but also capable of great kindness. For each set of parents, Birdie, Lu', and P.T. could be a test in patience.

Many other parents forbade their progeny from associating with the boys, whom they considered criminals in training, yet because of their powerful charisma, some kids were magnetically attracted to them. They were clever too. They snuck downstairs to the church cafeteria during Sunday Mass and hit the donut case before the other parishioners adjourned for coffee and donuts. Consequently, the nuns had to put the hammer down on the lads frequently, which inevitably made them more determined. They were more than just juvenile delinquents; they were also budding scholars who performed well in the classroom.

They were, in a word, precocious. The nuns, who knew they had their work cut out for them, were particularly good at interrogation. For the uninitiated, their tactics led to big trouble. As a result, the boys became consummate liars and world-class-level bullshit artists. "They don't pay us enough to monitor those troublemakers," said one nun in jest.

Birdie met Sally Bauer during the summer of 1969 near the soapbox derby track at Mt. Tabor Park, a nearly two-hundred-acre preserve located squarely in the middle of East Portland. An extinct volcanic cinder cone in the Boring Lava Field, Mt. Tabor predated the major Cascade volcanoes and had been inactive for about three hundred thousand years. Cloaked with tall firs, Mt. Tabor rose like a green oasis to the 641-foot summit above the surrounding neighborhoods.

Small reservoir on Mt. Tabor looking north

The grassy area below the soapbox derby track was a popular spot for playing Frisbee while sharing a half gallon of Bali Hai, a sweet, fruity wine that was popular with the girls. Sally immediately caught Birdie's eye. She had a beautiful, round face with sparkling, green eyes and long, brown hair that flowed to the small of her back. For her part, she was attracted to Birdie as well, but while a handsome lad in his own right, her interest was more about his intellect and sense of humor. The two made quite a pair together, and after a few weeks, they agreed to "go steady," as was the custom of the day.

For the boys, Mt. Tabor Park was headquarters, their Sherwood Forest. "We own this park," Lu' was fond of saying, which in a way was true. Though none held the deed, they qualified as certifiable squatters, considering how much time each spent there. Most lived within a block or two of this park with the best views of the Cascade Mountains, and most of Portland, with overlooks galore. To the west, the view featured incredible sunsets framed by the downtown skyline—with Portland's tallest buildings prominently positioned—and the West Hills. To the east, the scenery featured stunning views of large, glaciated stratovolcanoes: Mt. Hood, Mt. St. Helens, and Mt. Adams.

The taller, southern half of Mt. Tabor was preserved as a city park in 1909, while the northern half became a neighborhood. The homes near the park featured a hodgepodge of architectural styles from 1880s Queen Annes to 1960s high school shop class: Colonial revivals, English Tudor, and English cottage-style bungalows.

The boys initially walked and biked to the park. Later, they drove and parked their cars at the summit in the evenings—their own personal Inspiration Point, a gathering place where they could hatch plans and, in rare moments, stash their booty. Ultimately, the park became a place to drink adult beverages and consume illicit drugs. It was their haven—a place to hang out, swim in the reservoirs in the summer, play football, get into fights, and hide from cops and parents.

The park also was one of the few places to enjoy some privacy with a girl. Birdie and Sally had been together for nearly three years, and they had discussed the prospect of marriage though not seriously. Sally had yet to graduate from high school, but that date was coming soon—June 1972. Birdie picked up Sally one day, and the pair drove to the summit of Mt. Tabor. As they observed the twinkling lights of downtown Portland, Birdie pulled out an engagement ring and asked, "So what do you think, Sal?" They were in love—or so they thought—and her answer was a definitive "yes!" This special moment would signal the beginning of the end for Birdie and Sally.

Birdie's experiences with females were not unlike many others. On his way home from his first grade class at OLPS, a neighborhood kid named Cathy Byers hailed him. She was a year older, and Birdie showed deference to her status as his elder and complied.

"I want to tell you a secret," she said, not betraying her intentions.

As Birdie drew close, Cathy planted a kiss squarely on his cheek. Mortified, he hastened home without saying a word. *Yuck*! he thought. His face felt flushed. *How embarrassing. It's one thing to be kissed by your mom or your grandma, but a girl?* It wouldn't be the last time he was fooled by the fairer sex.

Initially, he kept the incident to himself, but eventually he opened up to his mom. "You'll be okay," she said. "There are worse things than being kissed by a girl."

"Please don't tell anybody," he begged her.

She said something like "Mum's the woid." He had no idea what she was talking about.

"Please!"

"Don't worry. It's just between you and me," she said.

Birdie knew she would keep her word, Good Catholic that she was. His mystery surrounding girls continued to grow, and his fascination with the fairer sex belied any sense of a latency period, but at that point, he wouldn't know what to do with a girl if he caught one.

The boys had a sense of adventure, especially when it came to heart-pounding hijinks and salacious sex. When the latter wasn't available, which was most of the time, the former would do nicely. They had a knack for finding trouble. They didn't have to work too hard, because trouble frequently found them. They were slippery sorts, often able to elude police and other authority figures with quick-witted resourcefulness and guile. Lightning rods for trouble, they were considered the scourge of the neighborhood. When they weren't able to talk their way out of trouble, they were skilled in the chase. Time and again, they escaped the clutches of Portland's finest.

On the search for some LSD, a psychedelic drug popular at the time, the boys scored a few tabs of "orange sunshine" at Laurelhurst Park, a popular marketplace to buy and sell illicit drugs. Their common ploy to stay out all night was telling their parents they were having a sleepover at Lu's house. With so many kids already around the Moriarity home, nobody noticed a few more in the basement.

After a long evening of wild hallucinations and aimless wandering, they settled in for what they considered deep-seated discussions of the meaning of life on the front lawn of a neighbor. As they spoke, the porch light on the house switched on and off repeatedly. The boys paid little heed to the apparent signs of trouble. Suddenly, they noticed a black-and-white cruiser—Portland police officers—headlights off, proceeding with stealth. The cop car was attempting to sneak up on the unsuspecting, drug-addled trio.

Spotting them, Lu' yelled, "Cops!" and they scattered like cockroaches exposed to light, fleeing toward a cedar fence, their only logical escape route. Hitting the boards simultaneously, they flattened the aging wall like a pancake and dispersed in different directions. Birdie doubled back into an adjacent yard and hid at the base of a laurel thicket, hoping the police would follow the others. Fortunately, his instincts were correct, but he dared not try to return to the Moriarity household and the safety of their basement too quickly. Cowering in the thick bushes, he could hear the cops lamenting the loss of their quarry. The LSD hallucinations were intense, and it was all Birdie could do to suppress his heavy breathing.

After about two hours in the laurel bush, Birdie made his move, carefully inching back to safety. When he arrived at the Moriarity basement, he rested on the couch for a while. Eventually, he had to pee, but he feared using the basement toilet would awaken someone upstairs. Quickly, he located a Folgers Coffee can and peed freely, but with the hallucinations, it appeared that the bottom of the can had dropped to the level of the concrete floor. *Weird*, he thought. It was still dark, so he resumed his position on the couch.

Meanwhile, P.T. and Lu' had run a couple blocks farther and hid under a parked car in a driveway. At times, they felt like they were in plain sight of the police, and they almost gave up twice, but they held their ground, and the police inexplicably departed. Both arrived back at the Moriarity basement at dawn, and all was well. Or was it? "Shit," said Lu'. "I lost my wallet."

The police had located the errant leather, of course, and appeared at the Moriarity residence later that morning. Confronted about how he had lost his wallet, Lu' did what he did best: convincingly lie through his teeth. The boys in blue left empty-handed.

In another incident following a concert at Mt. Hood Community College, Birdie and Lu' spotted a pair of large speakers hanging in the vestibule, ripe for the taking. Brazen thieves, they pulled the speakers off the wall and proceeded to the parking lot with their booty, snickering the whole way. Their celebration was short lived, because a pair of security guards awaited them in the parking lot.

"Hey, where are you going with those speakers?" asked one.

"Nowhere," said Birdie, as Lu' handed them to the surprised security guards. Lu' and Birdie then sprinted toward the adjacent avenue and the endless hayfields beyond.

The rent-a-cops, shocked by this bit of derring-do, gave chase, but they were no match for the boys in a footrace. "Stop, or we'll shoot!" yelled one.

Birdie and Lu' weren't fooled. The chase was over. They disappeared into the tall grass and had eluded the authorities once again.

Most of the boys were notorious kleptomaniacs who would pilfer just about anything, and on one occasion, they spotted an opportunity for one of the more epic heists of their lives. Birdie, Neil, and Steve Jackson devised a plan to steal a cigarette machine from Robin's burger joint on Eighty-Second Avenue in broad daylight.

They had been casing the joint for several weeks, and the plan was simple. Birdie would distract the servers while the other two wheeled the heavy cigarette machine over to Neil's getaway van. The caper went smoothly until they arrived at the van. They had underestimated the weight of the machine and hailed Birdie to help. As they wheeled the machine away, none of the shocked drive-in customers bothered to get out of their cars to stop the boys, who struggled to lift the three-hundred-pound beast into the back of Neil's panel truck. The adrenaline flowed like a roaring spring creek. Once in the back, they quickly skedaddled to the Moriarity basement. Though locked with hasp and padlock, it would be no match for a crowbar. Lu', who had joined them in the basement, sprung the lock, spraying coins and cigarettes everywhere.

"Shmocks!" exclaimed Neil, "this is outrageous."

After cleaning out all the change and smokes, the next step was to dispose of the machine. They couldn't leave it in the Moriarity basement, where it would be discovered by the parents.

"What should we do with this piece of shit?" asked Birdie.

"Let's dump it in the parking lot at OLPS," said Lu'. And so it was. In hindsight, the heist wasn't for the smokes or even the money, for that matter. It was for the rush.

As teenagers, the boys had become skilled hooligans, but they didn't start out that way. All were born into stable families with loving parents, so what happened? How did it all begin? How did three altar boys turn out to be so contrarian? Birdie attributed their morphed mentality to the nuns and the general draconian atmosphere at

OLPS, one of extreme repression. That's the short answer; the real reasons were much more complex. True, Catholic school could be a complete drag, partly because it was an artificial construct. OLPS took students down a path to a crossroads; one route was learning and education leading to success in life, but the other direction could lead to a life of ignorance and untamed chaos. Choose the wrong fork, the reasoning went, and you might become lost in the woods of wild childhood and never recover. Such was the myth that Catholic schooling silently endorsed: the child without proper education was doomed to a life that was less than ideal. To mitigate that possibility, orthodox religion and rigorous schooling were imposed on their young lives, and in the case of OLPS, the nuns enacted ritual and routine in a radical intervention.

This environment might explain why the approach made such an impression on the boys—sometimes traumatically. The concept was that school would help them overcome their childhood rawness, keeping their animal instincts at bay while encouraging their higher human capabilities. Students were embarking on a journey of academic achievement, and the framework was indoctrination into a set of cultural practices with the purpose of maintaining the system of Catholic morals and principles. That premise cast new light on the expression of "behaving in class."

The idea was to act in a way that corresponded with the class structure of society, not just the classroom. At home, they might receive personal attention when something went wrong such as comfort from a parent or grandparent to make things right. At school, their world was transformed: no more soft furnishings or carefree days of fun. Instead, students traded the couch and endless playtime at home for hard tables, desks, and the relentless metronome of a school timetable. Home featured its own routines like dinner and bedtime and prohibited activities like eating on the couch. At school, however, they encountered a whole new legislature that appeared magisterial and perplexing. Having had free rein at home, even though bound by a set of domestic codes, OLPS students dealt with a more rigid structure.

Most tyrannical of all was the figure of the Mother Superior, who doubled as the principal. Her minions were the nuns, an androgynous group of people because of bulky, flowing habits and generally disagreeable natures. Most students became keenly aware of authoritarianism at OLPS, based primarily on the fact that the nuns were physically bigger. When they said "jump," the response they expected to hear was "how high?"

If they didn't get the answer they were looking for from a student, the situation could lead to further punishment. Everyone, even nonviolators who watched in horror, assumed that the Roman Catholic Church officially sanctioned corporal punishment. The nuns who smacked Birdie and his ilk were known as Sisters of Charity—a cheap bit of irony. Of course, that's not to say that all nuns were created equal. Some, like Sister Marie, were truly benign and empathetic. Sister Josephine, who was truly disagreeable, at times could epitomize evil. Others, like Sister Antonia, were elderly and should not have been teaching at such an advanced age.

Not every nun resorted to physical violence. Most were adept at verbal abuse and could make a violator feel humiliated, even mortified, without the obvious evidence. The boys usually knew when they were in hot water with the nuns. For the more clueless students, the arbitrary nature of a broken rule, aligned with the authority of the teacher, generated a level of dread that was difficult to withstand. The only recourse was to store the episode in the memory banks for later. For the boys, the memory was retained for a more perverse purpose: retaliation.

Typically, there was little point to protest with the nuns. Indeed, protest itself would be evidence of disobedience. On the school grounds, it was a different dimension from home, as if one had just crossed the demilitarized zone (DMZ) from South Korea into North Korea. There was a need to observe rules that might be inadvertently flouted in this new jurisdiction or face the consequences for fighting, bullying, or other universally acknowledged crimes. The nuns established an atmosphere of fear and loathing to maintain control, leaving some students scarred for life while others found ways to cope within this structure. As a group, the nuns themselves were a paradox.

If there was an upside to the use of corporal punishment and verbal abuse, it was the spirit of camaraderie such behavior fostered among students. It was the class against the nuns all the way. Students were generally united in their defiance of authority and the Roman Catholic Church, for that matter. All felt every slap and not just the ones that fell across their own cheeks. Parents weren't much help; they'd been through similar situations as kids growing up in Catholic school. They were resigned to the fact that it was a way of life.

Basically, students were on their own, and that scenario made some tougher, wiser, and less trusting of people in power. It seemed odd to Birdie that the nuns would use intimidation to create order and improve test scores. It taught students about fear and humiliation. What fifth grader needs to learn about things like that? Another revelation for the younglings was that they were no longer special.

To make sure that point was clear, students were obliged to wear uniforms. Their individuality stripped away, students were just faces in the crowd. On the one hand, students were expected to take responsibility for themselves; on the other, they were just a number. Another paradox.

The boys were skilled at using this environment to their advantage. "That's wasn't me who peed in the drinking fountain. It was Tony!" Further eroding their sense of individuality, Catholic school meant a loss of privacy. The restroom stalls were open for all to see. If horseplay were to ensue, the nuns had no problem bursting in to restore order. Birdie always thought the nuns enjoyed those moments as opportunities to distribute further humiliation. Even using the toilet required asking for permission, as if the lives of children were common property. After years of schooling, Catholic school veterans are only now appreciating that fear is not conducive to learning even if it helps with discipline. In reality, the more emotionally settled, the more likely that the student will learn and ultimately succeed.

If the strict regimen at OLPS would alter the boys from within, other forces were at work from beyond. While the fifties were a decade of blandness, peace, and prosperity (to the relief of many who had weathered World War I, the Great Depression, and World War II), the sixties would be the antithesis of the previous decade. At the end of President Eisenhower's second term in 1960, his vice president, Richard M. Nixon, lost the presidency to the young, telegenic John F. Kennedy. Clearly, the next decade would be different but not in ways everybody would have envisioned.

The seeds of discontent had been sown, and the coming rebellion would not be denied. Individual rights would become the order of the day, championed by Dr. Martin

Luther King, Jr. and the civil rights movement. The failed attempt by the French to defeat communism in Vietnam would ultimately drag the United States into that quagmire, and by and large, Americans were not happy with the result.

The free speech movement at the University of California, Berkeley would further signal that Americans had a right to protest under the First Amendment of the US Constitution. Some observers believe this era was a classic nightmare where a rigid culture, unable to contain the demands for greater individual freedoms, broke free from the social constraints by extreme deviation from the norm. Birdie and the boys were more than happy to go along for the ride.

CHAPTER TWO

Descent into Darkness

Spring 1972: March began ominously for Birdie; he received his notice from the local draft board. "Dear Mr. McInnes, We have found you to be in good physical health and have classified you as 1A and fit for military service..." This missive would become a harbinger, a bad sign of things to come.

One night, Birdie, Sally, Neil Moriarity, and his girlfriend, Eidleigh, attended an all-night showing of James Bond flicks featuring Sean Connery at the Family Drive-In in Tigard, a small suburb of Portland. Appropriately packing the accoutrements necessary for such an event—plenty of beer and weed—Birdie was at the wheel of his 1962 GMC panel truck. He picked up Sally and headed out for the drive-in. Sally's mom often commented to Sally, with more than a hint of disgust, that the vehicle was a "bedroom on wheels." Neil and Eidleigh parked their car outside the drive-in, and they jumped in with Birdie and Sally so to pay for only one vehicle.

At the time, drive-in movies theaters, much like an endangered species, were on a path to extinction. In an effort to differentiate from traditional theaters, drive-ins staged all-night movie-thons. It was a clever bit of marketing for the drive-ins, but the technique delayed their demise by only a few years.

Birdie backed the vehicle into a slot and opened the back doors, and they all got comfortable for a six-hour medley of *Dr. No, From Russia With Love,* and *Goldfinger.* Birdie's GMC was the perfect vehicle for such an event, because they could flip the rear doors open, hook up two speakers on each door, and voila, enjoy a full view of the screen while remaining hidden from vehicles on either side. As the foursome sat in back of the Jimmy, knocking back 16-ounce Heidelbergs in keg bottles, smoking herb and cigarettes, the urge for mischief was too much for the boys.

At one point during the first show, Neil and Birdie excused themselves to take a pee. The restroom, located in a building at the center of the drive-in, housed a projection room and refreshment stand. After relieving themselves, the boys saw the back door was open directly to the refreshments. They couldn't resist. They grabbed two cases of Turkish taffy, and hearing someone yell, "Hey, you two, stop!" they dropped the cases and sprinted back to their vehicle, huffing and puffing.

"What's going on?" said Eidleigh.

"Oh, nothing," Neil said. "Let's get the hell out of here."

Sally was already passed out in the back. As he considered having Sally's company to keep him awake on the drive home, Birdie snickered to himself, thinking of the hint of disgust in Sally's mom's voice when she referred to the vehicle as a "bedroom on wheels." Realizing it was nearly 2:00 a.m. and it would take longer to wake her than not, they exited the theater. Birdie dropped Neil and Eidleigh off at their car, and he continued down US 99 toward Portland. His heart sank when he spotted the telltale red flashing lights of a police car in his mirror. *Shit, the cops,* he thought, his sphincter tightening. As the policeman approached the vehicle, Birdie's heart pounded. He was unsure of what to say or do.

"Yes, officer?"

"Get out!" the policeman demanded.

Sally, passed out in the back, was oblivious to the hubbub. As Birdie exited his vehicle, the cop hit Birdie on his forehead with a large flashlight, knocking him to the ground. Quickly, the stocky officer put a wrestling move on Birdie and handcuffed him behind his back. Rousing Sally, he conducted a quick search of the vehicle, finding the beer and weed but also methamphetamine in Sally's jean pockets. Both were transported to the Washington County jail in Hillsboro, the opposite direction from home. Birdie was incarcerated, and Sally, only sixteen, was released into the custody of her parents.

Birdie was charged as a minor in possession of alcohol, possession of marijuana, possession of a controlled substance, and statutory rape (Sally's jeans were found to be unbuttoned). Birdie was obliged to remain incarcerated for the entire weekend. His cellmates were career criminals charged with attempted murder and armed robbery. He spent the weekend playing Scrabble with his cellmates before his mom could post bail on Monday.

"What are you in for?" one asked.

"You know, I'm not really sure," Birdie said. "Apparently, the drive-in theater owner called the police. But they found speed on my girlfriend, and I was the one charged with possession."

"Speed, huh? That's a felony."

"Yes, I've heard."

Once charged and arraigned, Birdie was released. Back at his house, his dad greeted him with a disgusted "welcome home, jailbird." His mom, more forgiving and more interested in his welfare, asked if he was okay. "I would have left him in jail," his dad groused.

Anticipating legal issues, his mom called a childhood friend and lawyer, Don Simonsen, who agreed to take the case.

"Mom," Birdie said, "these charges are bogus. Yes, I'm guilty of the beer and the weed, but the speed was Sally's."

"Never mind that. We'll leave it to Don," she said reassuringly.

The only good news was that while awaiting trial, Birdie's draft status was postponed indefinitely until his legal situation could be resolved.

The amorous advances by Cathy Byers aside, Birdie did not experience his first real kiss until a few years later during one of his nocturnal wanderings about the neighborhood. It was trendy for many at OLPS, particularly those in their teenage years, to sneak out in the middle of the night after their parents had retired for the day. Birdie would meet with P.T., Lu', and their ilk to rendezvous with the girls of OLPS for innocent talk, usually at Mt. Tabor Park. The meetings were rife with excitement and intrigue, mostly because they were conducted illicitly by all concerned and required timing and stealth. Some had an easier time of it than others because their parents were out of town overnight, divorced (it was much easier to fool one parent than two), or worked graveyard.

Birdie had none of those advantages; both parents were home every night. To make matters worse, he had four younger siblings who could "spill the beans" at any time. Fortunately, he and Emile had an advantage: their bedrooms were in the basement with a back door ready at hand—their own escape route to the world.

One night, plans were hatched for one of their nocturnal meetings with the girls. Participants would meet at 2:00 a.m. at Mt. Tabor for a bit of fun and frivolity. The group, fairly evenly split between male and female, seemed larger than usual. Someone had invited several public school kids from the neighborhood, and the gaggle of teenagers meandered their way to the park.

The experience was not without potential hazards—you had to keep a wary eye out for cops on the prowl who could catch you for a curfew violation. Once in the park, however, it was easy to hide. Cops were no match for kids who knew the park well. There were too many good hiding places. Some in this group of public school kids were known locally as "mavos"—less affluent kids from a bordering neighborhood—but none of that mattered to anybody in the group. They were all in the adventure together. Birdie was attracted to one mavo girl by the name of Pinky Charleston. Very attractive, she had an exotic look because of her Filipino heritage. Someone had brought along some cheap Western beer, and all indulged.

After about two hours of aimless wandering and drinking, the time came to head home. As they bade their farewells, Pinky approached Birdie, kissed him squarely on his lips, and inserted her tongue into his mouth. For Birdie, the stimulating sensation would not be one he would soon forget. Her surprise kiss was unique, playful, and delicious, and Birdie felt light as a feather. Scientists describe the "French kiss" as the mutual impacting of the buccal membranes, creating an increased production of saliva and the activation of certain nerve endings.

Pinky's kiss was an extraordinary combination of the formal and the free, the ceremonious and the sensual, the ritualistic and the romantic. The experience had the effect of something significant without having been called for. Essentially spontaneous and gratuitous, it was purposeful without purpose. The kiss, sweet yet as tenuous as cotton candy, would provide the future key to a hitherto suspected but unknown secret garden of delights, yet it played on the margin between substance and nothingness; a kiss disappears in the having of it, like a puff of smoke.

Nonetheless, Birdie glowed the whole way home; he had experienced his first real French kiss! The sensation faded, however, once he returned to his house. Even though he had left the back door unlocked, the entry point was now secured, and the porch light was turned on. *I'm sure I left that light off*, he thought. Fortunately, he had left the bathroom window unlatched. He slipped in through the window without a sound and went to bed. Not long after he fell asleep, his dad yarded him out of bed like a Douglas fir on a logging site.

"Come with me," he demanded emphatically. He sat Birdie down at the kitchen table. "Where have you been?"

"Out" came the reply.

"I know that much. What were you doing?"

"Nothing," he uttered feebly.

"Okay, smart guy, you're going to sit here in this chair until you tell me where you were all night."

His dad had him situated over a barrel. Birdie was exhausted. Forced to remain awake but dying to sleep was the ultimate penalty. Birdie was pretty sure his dad had a sense of that sort of torture. After all, he had been a US marine, fighting in Korea, and had no doubt experienced nocturnal guard duty. Birdie imagined that other punishments would pale in comparison to being forced to remain awake when overcome by the need to sleep. After he fell off the chair a couple times, his dad could see that he had had enough.

"Go to bed," he said. "You look terrible."

Fortunately for Birdie, Don Simonsen had considerable legal skills. An experienced barrister, he had succeeded in defending antiwar demonstrators accosted by police at moratorium marches in protest of the Vietnam War in downtown Portland. Simonsen learned the cop who struck Birdie on the side of his head with his flashlight had a track record of serial violence with youth. For the errant police officer, already skating on thin ice because of his overly aggressive nature, Birdie's case would be the last straw. Before the case even went to court, the cop resigned from the force in the Washington County Sheriff's Department and joined the Marine Corps.

"We're in luck," said Simonsen when he met with Birdie and his mom. "The key witness for the prosecution is no longer available to testify. The county has agreed to drop the statutory rape and possession of a controlled substance charges, both felonies. We just need to plead guilty to minor in possession of alcohol and the marijuana charge."

"Do we have any other options?" Birdie asked.

"Not really," he replied.

"When will we know the outcome?" his mom inquired.

"Probably in a few months," Simonsen said. "Try to keep your nose clean until then."

Meanwhile, Birdie, now a freshman at Mt. Hood Community College and studying journalism, refocused on his studies. Many of their group remained conscientious students, although Birdie and Lu' were the only ones with some semblance of direction. Birdie wanted to be a newspaper reporter. Lu', coming from a family of educators, had a goal to become a teacher. P.T. wasn't sure, but he did well in his studies.

Aside from school, the boys were gainfully employed in part-time jobs in downtown Portland. Lu' was a parking attendant at City Center Parking, which he enjoyed because of the cool cars he'd park. His favorite? A Shelby GT with a 454-cubic-inch engine owned by the vice president of a local bank. P.T. worked at Western Union, delivering messages and packages to downtown businesses. Birdie's job as a mail room clerk was located next door to Western Union at Miller Freeman Publications, a magazine publisher.

Because they were all employed, the trio enjoyed a certain amount of financial freedom and independence, allowing them to purchase their first cars. Lu' bought a '57 Ford Fairlane while Birdie opted for a sparkling, blue Volkswagen Bug. P.T. had the most unusual vehicle of all: a DKW, a two-cycle vehicle from Germany that ran on a combination of oil and gas. A strange-looking automobile, the beast looked like a World War I German armored vehicle with an unusual engine sound resembling a power tool.

None of the vehicles were necessarily reliable, but they were serviceable. Despite Birdie's status with the courts, he couldn't avoid trouble with the crew he ran with. Driving by Safeway, the boys spotted cardboard cases of cantaloupes ripe for picking. With vandalism on their mind, they plucked a few melons from the bin and drove to the soap box derby track at Mt. Tabor, where numerous parked cars provided handy targets. As they passed a string of cars, it was "bombs away" at one particular vehicle. Unfortunately, P.T. recognized the driver of the car as a notorious tough guy at his high school. Too late. The melons found their target.

"Oh, shit," bellowed P.T. "That's Mark Freeman. If he catches us, he's going to beat the holy hell out of all of us."

"Punch it," yelled Lu'.

Punching it wasn't an option in a DKW, possibly the least powerful automobile on the planet. The boys needed divine intervention to escape this time. Freeman had a cherry '56 Chevy with a souped-up 283-cubic-inch V8 with a four-barrel carburetor. It would be no contest; the boys were as good as dead. Fortunately, P.T. was a clever driver and able to pass a few cars due to the small size of the DKW. They quickly put some distance between their getaway car and Freeman. Wheeling as quickly as possible to the entrance of the park, P.T. took a right turn onto Sixtieth Avenue. Unfortunately, he made a critical error in judgment; they immediately took another right, doubling back into the park straight into a dead end.

"Trapped like rats," muttered Lu' with resignation.

"Let's back up and get out of here!" Birdie said.

As P.T. frantically backed up, he clipped the car parked on his right. Panicked, he backed the other direction, hitting the parked car on his left. "Oh, man, we need to move quickly. This guy will kill us when he catches us." Finally turned around, the boys slowly crept back down the street, anticipating a showdown.

"You boys ready for a bit of fisticuffs?" asked P.T.

"We'll have no choice," replied Lu'.

Incredibly, when they arrived back at Sixtieth Avenue, Freeman was gone. Anticipating an ambush, he apparently had been wary to follow the boys up the dead end. Perhaps he didn't like the odds. Relieved, the lads had once again escaped fate. "What a rush!" exclaimed Birdie.

Despite often making life miserable for others, what they didn't know then but would emphatically learn later was the concept of karma: an action for an action. If the action was made with good intentions, positive things would result. If the action was bad, woe be to that person. The boys would come to understand this concept over time the hard way. Karma was a patient gangster.

No doubt the nuns at OLPS, who comprised the majority of the teaching staff and administration at the coeducational school, had their hands full with younglings with raging hormones. In the sixties, kids seemed to mature increasingly sooner due to the more permissive era. By seventh or eighth grade, their hormones were raging, making it even more difficult for the androgynous Sisters of Charity to maintain order. The nuns faced the unenviable of suppressing the burgeoning sexuality of their charges. Their efforts were slightly more successful with the girls, or so the thinking went.

At first, the nuns attempted to rationalize with young females. "You can't get your virginity back once it's gone," they said. "Don't give into emotional blackmail either. If a boy says 'you would if you loved me' or 'everyone else is doing it,' don't give in." When logic didn't work, the nuns resorted to good old Catholic guilt. "If you lose your virginity, you'll lose all your self-respect." Worse, they said, "You could become pregnant and ruin your life." In the most severe cases, the warning was basically this: "If you lose your virginity before you marry, you'll regret it for the rest of your life and then burn in hell."

The nuns themselves knew a thing or two about virginity. For them, Catholicism was a cult of virginity. Of course, the nuns made easy targets for jokes and sexual innuendo coming from ill-mannered students, yet they all seemed to take their virginity seriously. Some were well past menopause anyway. As the nuns espoused in religion class, Mary, the mother of God, effaced herself in deference to the glory of God. In other words, her virginity provided a form of self-sacrifice.

In the New Testament, Mary is quoted thusly, "I make myself small so you can be great." That said, it stood to reason that to lose one's virginity was to sacrifice the potential for sacrifice ("sacrifice" meaning "making sacred"). No doubt this self-sacrifice was what motivated the nuns to remain celibate. To the nuns, losing their virginity would not only defile the body but distract from prayer. Their chastity would provide the opportunity to offer themselves up to God in such a holy fashion. In other words, carnal knowledge would be a distraction from their true purpose: devotion to God.

Carnality is, of course, the ultimate body experience, one in which reason is cast aside in the name of intimacy and pleasure. Why should first-time sex be approached with all of one's cognitive faculties on high alert? Why, despite all the solemn warnings and caveats (such as the risk of pregnancy and the fear and anxiety of wasting a sacred truth), were teenagers so focused on sex as a rite of passage?

For the nuns, the timing wasn't helping their cause. The burgeoning mores of the "free love" movement of the sixties were beginning to influence the younglings. For some, corporal pleasure was indeed strong enough to outweigh all the dastardly disadvantages, and the desire to have sex is the most compelling of human urges. Regardless, most teenagers in the sixties ignored the nun's advice directed their way, primarily with the inclusion of an ever-expanding list of birth control methods such as "the pill." Turns out, even the nuns at OLPS—particularly the younger ones—were not immune from such compelling urges. Many eventually abandoned their vows, married, and had children of their own.

By late spring, the walls of authority were narrowing, and antagonists of all stripes were drawing a bead on Birdie: his parents, Sally's parents, his teachers, the local draft board, and perhaps most worrisome, the police. Several subsequent incidents with the cops led to a watershed experience that would alter his life.

Birdie and Lu' were party to a dope deal unceremoniously interrupted. Perched at the top of Mt. Tabor where they could see approaching traffic, the pair had just purchased a quarter pound of Mexican weed when they spotted a black-and-white unit with Portland's finest speeding to the top. Without thinking, they jumped in another car with buddies and made their escape, leaving the weed in the glove box of Birdie's latest vehicle, a 1953 Chevy.

Unfortunately, they left the car, known as the Green Weenie, exposed and unlocked. Escaping the police was the easy part. How to get the Green Weenie back would be another matter. Nobody knew how the car came to be known as the Green Weenie, because its color was actually pale blue, but much like an adopted dog, the name came along with the car as part of the deal. "Do you think they'll search the car?" asked Birdie. "What should I do?"

"Only one thing to do," replied Lu'. "Report it stolen."

When he arrived home, Birdie reported that his car had been stolen.

The next day, a couple of plainclothes police officers arrived at Birdie's family home. "Is Robert McInnes at home? We have a few questions about his car."

Birdie's siblings were well trained to inform any military recruiters or police officers that he wasn't home. "Nope," said Emile. "We're not sure where he is."

"Well," they said, "here's our number. Have him give us a call." The truth was that Birdie was laying low with Lu' and P.T.

Briefly free from the restraints of living at home, the situation continued to deteriorate for Birdie. Busted again as a minor in possession of alcohol at a high school football jamboree, Birdie and Neil spent the night incarcerated in the Multnomah County jail. Birdie's dad refused to bail him out, as usual, so his mom rode the bus downtown to spring him from detention. He called Lu' for a ride home.

Meanwhile, Sally's parents, and Sally herself, had run out of patience with Birdie. "He's incorrigible," Sally's mom told her. It wasn't the first, or the last, time someone used that term to describe Birdie. Sally too grew weary of Birdie's antics. While he was in Lincoln City for a month, making amends with his dad by helping him work on his beach house, Sally dated Steve Hill, a fellow classmate of Birdie's from OLPS. She was smitten with Steve, and the two unabashedly appeared at all the usual haunts. Birdie's friends knew about the affair, but they kept the matter quiet.

Eventually, P.T. and the others devised a note using cut-out words from magazines and sent the letter to Birdie surreptitiously. Heartbroken, Birdie confronted Sally and Steve separately in their own homes to inform them of his discovery. Contrite, they both fessed up to the affair. Steve, a championship-caliber high school wrestler, was nervous and visibly shaken. Despite his size advantage over Birdie, Steve cowered when confronted and apologized.

Sally was matter-of-fact. She admitted, unremorsefully, that she was having the affair. "There's nothing you can do about it. Sorry. I've found new love." Sally returned all his gifts except for one; she kept the engagement ring and sold it for cash at a pawn shop on Grand Avenue on the lower east side of Portland. Sally, the erstwhile love of his life, had moved on.

Soon Birdie moved on as well. As far as he was concerned, Sally had become the girl from yesterday. Indeed, it wasn't long before he started to enjoy his newfound freedom, dating Sally's cousin, Cheryl Bauer.

Most in a position of authority—mainly Birdie's parents and teachers—were at a loss to explain the wild and untamed nature of the boys. They were smart, intelligent kids. Why were they so rambunctious and daring in finding ways to flout authority?

Birdie attributed the condition to the nuns and their repressive ways. Not every nun resorted to physical, emotional, or mental abuse, but the ones who did had established a pervasive atmosphere of low-grade dread among students. Offenses ranged from simply "talking back" to more serious transgressions such as swearing, fighting, fooling around in church, throwing snowballs, and other mischief, mostly kid stuff.

Because the nuns had their own mysterious criteria for punishment, not to mention unfathomable moods, the way they meted out punishment was nerve wracking. They were, in short, unpredictable and random. A smart remark might merit the evil eye one day and a slap across the face the next. Some kids became targets for more than their fair share of abuse. Others came from broken homes; they had been sent to Catholic school to help assure a straight and narrow path.

Some, however, could not contain their outrage at the treatment they received. When hit by nuns, they overreacted by crying, yelling, or stomping out of the classroom, thus establishing themselves as easy targets for future discipline. The rest learned to take their punishment without flinching. Though it was rare to see a female get slapped across the face, some poor girls got rapped across the knuckles with a ruler when violating a rule. Unlike some of the poor schmucks who consistently drew the wrath of the women in habits, Birdie and his friends adapted to this heavy-handed environment quickly. They all became adept at lying with conviction. Even as youngsters, the boys couldn't resist finding trouble.

To keep them occupied in the summertime, their parents required them to enroll at OLPS for harvest work in the berry and bean fields surrounding Portland where they could earn money to help pay for school clothes and supplies. During the summer, students met at OLPS at 5:00 a.m. on weekdays and rode the school bus to various fields. In June, the harvest was strawberries, and they typically picked at Mr. Kato's Strawberry Farm in southeast Portland. The girls at the school were superior pickers; they worked quickly and diligently throughout the day. Some could net more than twenty dollars in one day.

The boys were considerably less successful, primarily because they were slow and preoccupied with other activities like throwing strawberries, meeting girls, and listening to music. Essentially, they were slackers who were more inclined toward shenanigans and hooliganism. Mr. Kato had a name for these characters: "little gangsters." He was right, of course, and Birdie, Lu', P.T., Neil, and the rest were all part of that group. Nonetheless, Mr. Kato liked the boys, though he was likely relieved when they moved on to other endeavors like paper routes and other part-time jobs.

The boys were adrenaline junkies. They would lurk at the entryway at the top of the bike racks at OLPS and hone their skills in the art of the dodge. After dark, they taunted passing cars in an effort to initiate a chase. About one in four would take the bait. When a car stopped and backed up, the boys took off at a full sprint down the narrow alley behind the school. It was about a one hundred-yard dash down the narrow causeway with no escape portals until the convent, where three new escape routes awaited.

One night, they picked the wrong guy: a fellow on motorcycle. Big mistake. While cars were unable to negotiate the slim causeway, a motorcycle had no such constrictions. When the boys bolted, the motorcycle pursued them at full speed. Their shadows reflected against the side of the convent by the headlight, adding visual urgency to their plight. Sprinting with unbridled enthusiasm, all bolted in separate directions at the convent. The motorcycle rider came up empty-handed that evening. The group gathered once the motorcyclist had had his fun. "What a rush!" Lu' exclaimed.

Their ability to cope in an era of changing mores was more than just their propensity for shenanigans. Other forces were at work in the early sixties: the social and political hailstorm pounded American society from every direction. The upheaval during those turbulent years upset long-held notions of everything including politics, race relations, marriage and family, and the role of women in society. The counterculture began to surface.

The impact on a new generation was enormous. Fortunately, OLPS instructors taught students the importance of hard work and a discipline to study. American society would survive in the face of this cultural upheaval, as would the boys. When they all eventually—and perhaps inevitably—transferred to public schools to finish high school, they were well prepared academically.

They were simply a product of their environment. In the sixties, most adults smoked cigarettes and, in the case of men, cigars or pipes. Some kids followed suit as soon as they could get away with it. The drinking age was twenty-one, but more than a few underage youngsters were drinking long before then. For the boys, finding someone to buy a bottle of beer, wine, or liquor was easy. They could then adjourn to the top of Mt. Tabor to imbibe. High school students could obtain their driver's license at age sixteen, and some had their own cars.

In the previous decade, renegade images of Marlon Brando and Lee Marvin in *The Wild Ones* and James Dean in *Rebel without a Cause* popularized the dubious allure of the "tough guy" image in movies and television that featured urban teenage males. The female equivalent was probably tight skirts topped with a tight sweater. These images were merely previews of coming attractions. As dull and boring as the fifties seemed with President Eisenhower at the helm of America, the sixties became the opposite. The civil rights and women's movements and the Vietnam War spawned a whole revolution. The boys unwittingly became subsumed in this hopelessly lost and restless generation.

Unlike antiauthoritarian movements of previous eras, the youth of the country moved beyond the focus of life that had preoccupied their parents, and most engaged in the dissonance of the era. As the decade progressed, widespread social tensions were palpable, and differing perspectives of the American Dream developed. The divide aligned along generational lines, and new cultural forms emerged that were reflected in the literature, music, and art of the day. In the broadest sense, changing mores grew from a confluence of people, events, circumstances, and advancing technology, providing intellectual and social catalysts for rapid change during the sixties.

Although the nuns at OLPS could be difficult for many students, they did one thing well: they knew how to teach. All were highly educated. Many attended summer school to obtain advanced degrees. Forbidden from earthly temptations, most nuns, aside from praying, spent their time reading and teaching. The younglings who were lucky enough to attend parochial school were obliged to learn how to read, and read they did, moving from basic readers to more sophisticated tomes.

Before reaching middle school, those who paid attention knew the eight parts of speech and could diagram sentences as well as recite the auxiliary verbs and personal pronouns by heart. Birdie became a voracious reader with an innate ability to memorize words and their meanings. Those who served as altar boys also memorized phrases in Latin, because in those days, Mass was conducted in that now-defunct language. Students also could take Spanish, which Birdie did, and from living with his gramma, he had developed a working knowledge of Italian. After completing the required courses in Latin, Italian, and Spanish at Jesuit High School, he was proficient in each.

In grade school, Birdie plucked a copy of *Catcher in the Rye* by J. D. Salinger from his dad's bookshelf and, fascinated, read the tale in its entirety one weekend. The book, written for a previous generation, was a transformative experience, and Birdie wouldn't be the only one affected. The controversial novel, published in 1951, resonated with other teenagers across America in the sixties with its themes of angst and alienation.

The protagonist, Holden Caulfield, became an icon of restiveness and rebellion for an entire generation of youth. Still in prep school, Holden is intelligent but an outsider among his peers. He reads books like *Out of Africa* yet is dismissed from his prep school. He can't seem to click with anybody and is occasionally beaten by classmates. Nonetheless, he maintains an air of self-determination and ventures to New York City on his own, staying in a seedy, run-down hotel. Preoccupied with losing his virginity, Holden visits Greenwich Village, where he agrees to consort with a prostitute. When he has second thoughts about the endeavor, Holden tells her he just wants to talk. Annoyed, she leaves and returns with her pimp, who punches Holden in the stomach. His only friend in the world appears to be his sister, Phoebe, and he alienates even her by suggesting that he will move out West.

Ultimately, it's a story of withdrawal as a form of self-protection. He feels trapped on "the other side" of life and continually searches for a world where he can feel like he belongs. Many denizens of OLPS could certainly relate to Holden's dilemma.

Birdie was also enamored with the other antiheroes of the era: Jay Gatsby from *The Great Gatsby*, Captain John Yossarian from *Catch-22*, and Randall Patrick McMurphy from *One Flew over the Cuckoo's Nest*, all books he consumed with enthusiasm in the late sixties.

In that decade, rebellion was in the air, and it wasn't confined to literature but extended to art and music. Birdie and his friends were swept away by the revolution in music, specifically the Beatles. While Elvis Presley would demonstrate how rebellion could be fashioned in eye-popping style, the Beatles exemplified how style could impact a cultural revolution. Their arrival in the American consciousness announced that music—and the times—would be changing, and the Beatles would lead the way.

Other bands would contribute to the sense of an emerging scene including the Kinks, the Who, the Animals, and the Rolling Stones, with music just as vital and even more aggressive. Birdie's dad hated the Beatles. As someone who enjoyed the strains of the Ray Conniff Singers and Mantovani, his dad suggested lighter fare for Birdie like the Beach Boys, a wholesome American band that sang about a youth culture of surfing, cars, and romance. Birdie enjoyed the music of the Beach Boys, but it was the Beatles who really captured his imagination. He was obsessed, saving up his money to buy every record he could. Birdie also loved the music of the Who and the Rolling Stones. If Birdie's dad loathed the Beatles, he despised the Rolling Stones. He considered the band, which laced its songs with "druggie" lyrics, as coarse and vulgar.

In March, Birdie, Neil, Lu', and P.T. moved into a dilapidated three-story rental near Eighty-Second Avenue on the eastern edge of Portland. The cheap rent compensated for the lack of amenities. The spot quickly became a hangout for various and sundry buddies, girlfriends, and other dubious characters. The place was so foul (in both appearance and smell) that it soon became known as "Foul House," but it beat living at home, and the boys had free reign.

Later that month, local radio stations announced that the Rolling Stones would embark on a world tour, and Seattle would be part of the "tour America every three years" rotation that the group had established. Tickets would sell for "one day only" a couple of weeks before the show at the Seattle Center, site of the 1962 World's Fair.

At Foul House, the crew hatched plans to nominate Birdie and Neil, junior partners, to make the three-hour drive to Seattle in time to arrive at Seattle Center, wait in what would likely be a long line, and purchase tickets before the concert sold out. After a night of heavy drinking, Neil and Birdie popped a handful of amphetamine tablets and departed for Seattle in Neil's 1954 DeSoto Firedome, a five-ton boat of a vehicle. Somewhere along Interstate 5, probably near Chehalis, the DeSoto overheated and rolled to a dead stop on the side of the road. It was the middle of the night. Birdie thought, *We're screwed*.

"What now?" asked Birdie. "Not only will we not make it to Seattle in time to buy tickets, but we'll probably have to hitchhike back to Portland."

"Take it easy, Birdie," said Neil reassuringly. "We've got this."

Neil was mechanically gifted. Figuring that the car was overheated, he stretched the fan belt for a moment and then told Birdie, "Fire it up." Incredibly, the car started, and they were off again. By daylight, they had arrived at Seattle Center. The place was packed with waiting fans, so Birdie and Neil inched their way near the front of the pack and awaited the opening of the ticket booths. While waiting, several anxious ticket buyers passed out due to a lack of available oxygen. Those people were crowd-surfed over to the sidelines quickly. Finally, the booths opened, and the crowd pressed forward. With tickets in hand, Birdie and Neil fled back to Portland.

Three weeks later, a caravan left Foul House and ventured north, checking into the City Center Motel, a cheap hotel near the Seattle Center. Brandon Klumpf drew the short straw for checking into the dive, but he was a smart boy; he used P.T.'s name to register, which was a good thing, because their group pilfered pillows and towels. The gang congregated in Lu's room for a pre-function featuring some Henry's rhubarb wine, a high-potency concoction, along with a half dozen doobies, and then traipsed to the venue. The doors at Seattle Center opened at 8:00 p.m. like floodgates. Many in the group made it to the front row first, sliding into the stage base.

As more fans packed in, the group felt the crush of humanity behind them. Meanwhile, Birdie, Cheryl, and P.T. slowly eked their way to the front. The warm-up act, Stevie Wonder and his band, would have been worth the price of admission alone. The Rolling Stones took the stage, and a giant mirror hovered over the band on stage as they played a set from their new album, *Sticky Fingers*, before moving into their classic stuff. Everyone agreed: best concert ever.

That night, Cheryl and Birdie retreated to their room for some wild sex. Afterward, Cheryl informed Birdie that she actually had an orgasm. Just to insult Birdie, she said she envisioned fucking Mick Jagger during intercourse. He didn't care. He knew the end of his relationship with Cheryl was inevitable.

A couple of weeks later, a Portland radio station announced that Led Zeppelin would appear at the city's Memorial Coliseum. This time, everybody was on their own for tickets. Birdie and Cheryl had a pair, and most everybody else purchased tickets except for Neil. The anticipation for the concert was subdued compared to the Rolling Stones. At the show, Birdie was particularly captivated by "Stairway to Heaven," the band's hit. Sadly, the song would become prophesy.

The next morning, Craig Kubiak showed up at Birdie's and Neil's basement apartment. As white as a ghost, his face told the story. "Neil's dead," he said, horror-stricken.

"What happened?" asked Birdie, feeling the urge to throw up.

"He was t-boned in his car while heading out to the Columbia River for a houseboat party" came the reply.

The next two weeks were pure hell. One and all felt like they had lost a brother. Birdie, Craig, Chuck Schneider, Chris Oleson, and Billy Preston all served as pallbearers. The news would be too much for Eidleigh Fuller to bear. Later that week, she overdosed on pills, taking her own life.

Soon the denizens of Foul House would disperse to the winds. The watershed moment also would also herald the end of the road for Birdie and Cheryl. Much like with Sally, the writing was on the wall. For Birdie, one door had closed, but many more would soon open.

The McInnes brood didn't know it at the time, but their inherent mission in life was to torment Dear Old Dad. Unbeknown to one and all, it turned out old Dad had been messing around before he married Mom. Birdie received an unsolicited letter from a stranger who somehow had located him in East Portland. Her name was Julie Price, and her letter went like this.

Hi Birdie:

My name is Julie Price. I have learned that you are an aspiring writer, and I have a story that is sure to be of great interest to you. I will attempt to tell you the short version right now and see if you are interested in knowing more.

When my mother, Janine Phillips, had passed away, my mother's first cousin, Elizabeth, came to my house for a visit. She told me that my mother got pregnant in March of 1949, her senior year at Hillsboro High School in Portland, Oregon, and she was sent away to a foster home for unwed mothers. She had a baby boy on October 17, 1949, and gave him up for adoption. She didn't even get to hold him.

When I heard this news, I couldn't believe it, because I thought I was the eldest child in my family. I was born on August 1, 1953, and I have one younger sister and two younger brothers. It was a secret that no one knew, not even my father. When I discovered that I had a half-brother out there somewhere, I was so excited. All I could think about was finding him. I had no name to go by, nor did we know his father's name. I searched very hard and hired someone to help me.

I finally found him. He is a delightful and very intelligent man and has a wife, daughter, and two sons. His name is Oliver Wendall Smith, and he lives in Gresham, Oregon. I am quite certain that Oliver is your half-brother and that your father, Cyril William McInnes, is Oliver's biological father. There are so many more details I've gathered from my research that all add up. I would like to know if you or one of your siblings would be willing to talk or communicate in some way with me.

Oliver wants you all to know that he doesn't want anything from you but is happy to know about you. He'd love to meet you and talk with your father, if he is alive and willing to do so. I can fill you in on more details and send you photos if and whenever you would like. Please contact me anytime with a phone call at 252-4074. I hope to hear from you.

Warmly,
Julie

CHAPTER THREE

Fleeing the Maelstrom

Summer 1972: By summer, the heat intensified in more ways than one. Birdie's number was up, and his dad, a gruff Korean War veteran, suggested he join the marines like he himself had done. Robert Cameron McInnis had other ideas. His gramma, who had left Italy because the "smell of war" was "in the air" in 1912, as she described it, was opposed to the idea of Birdie joining the military and the prospect of winding up in Vietnam. His mom loathed the idea.

Birdie vividly remembered the horror of Jimbo. "I won't be joining a branch of the service," said Birdie. "I'll be heading to Canada soon."

"Out," shouted his dad abruptly, "out of this house!"

His mom tried to intervene, but Birdie went downstairs, collected a few things, and started to leave. On his way out the door, he announced, "Nope, I'm leaving Portland and heading to British Columbia."

His dad's lip started to quiver, a familiar sign of the potential for conflict. A preemptive tip, it was a nervous tick that suggested the unpleasantness to follow. It was as if adrenaline extracted from a hypothetical donor's pineal gland had been implanted into his Dad's lips, a warning that bad craziness was imminent. The hounds were about to be released. "I had friends who fought and died for this country," he cried, his eyes welling with tears.

"I just don't want to end up like Jimmy," Birdie said. On that note, he left.

Once again, he landed on the doorstep of P.T. and Lu's new apartment where he was welcomed with open arms. Before reporting for work at Crater Lake, P.T. took a one-month hiatus to visit his sister in Phoenix, Arizona, while Lu' and Birdie resumed their studies at Mt. Hood Community College. Birdie stayed in P.T.'s room, an upgrade from the Foul House.

While at Crater Lake, P.T. wrote home a couple of times.

Boys:
Just got your letter today. One of the idiots I live with delivered my mail about four days ago and threw it on top of my dresser, which is piled with clothes as usual. Today, when I was doing laundry, I uncovered your card and saw the invite to my brother's wedding (Harry's invite to 'his' wedding blew my mind) in Washington Park up in the West Hills. Baa-hoo! I will write him about the situation here. We pretty much have to work every day of the season, so my attendance at his wedding will be impossible. You boys can represent. I thought you guys wrote less than me, but I guess not. I can't get myself to do it half the time.

This is just the second letter I have written. I sent my mom a letter because she sent my Social Security check. In her letter, she enclosed envelopes, stamps, and paper. Grandma and Grandpa Talbot are going to disown me if I don't write them pretty soon. Glad to hear you guys are all staying drunk. You can rest assured that I'm doing my best, drinking a lot of hard stuff. We've been keeping well supplied. The FBI is here right now because someone stole $400 from the cafeteria store. I damn near had the day off last week to come to Portland for the Chicago concert, but some other punk on my crew got it off first, and I had to take his boat.

I got my butt chewed a couple of weeks ago because I made some anticoncession speeches on my tours. Some good friends of the boss on my boat heard my spiel, and they went and told him, so he called me into his office. He and the park superintendent took turns chewing my ass. The boss was drunk as usual, and the park superintendent can't stand him anyway.

There's some pretty cool park rangers up here. I'm really getting used to having cops around. There's one ranger, Bruce, who is a damn decent guy. He spends his summers at Crater Lake and his winters at Death Valley. Nice life. I smoke dope with him a lot. The other night, we had a concession-sponsored dance. We have them every two weeks or so from what I've heard. Everybody gets good and wasted.

After the band quit playing, we had some hash oil and pot, so we took our boat crew truck and started around the rim drive. About halfway around, Bruce came driving toward us in the ranger car. We all watched intently, and someone threw the lid in the glove box. Well, old Bruce turns around and pulls up behind us and throws the red flashers on. He comes over to the truck wearing a gun and the whole bit. They only have patrol duties twice a week, and they think it's a joke.

He walks over and asks me for my driver's license. The dudes in the back were freaking out. Bruce comes around the rig and opens the front passenger door and told the guy in front to move over. He got in and started going through the glove box. The dudes were going out of their minds at this point. When Bruce found the lid, he pulled out the papers and started rolling a joint, and we sat there smoking it with the flashers on the whole time.

I haven't seen a television or read a newspaper since I've been here. I feel really out of it. I hope my brother Mike isn't still messing around with those junkies. They scared me just looking at them. I heard Mike went to California. I wish he would have stopped here. When I'm not working, I'm either partying or sleeping. There's no in between. That's one reason why writing is so hard to fit in because it cuts into one of them, and they're all equally important.

We just had a free double kegger the other day with hamburgers and hot dogs for all the employees. We paid for it by selling our lunches every day. We bought two kegs and all the grub and still made $54 with more in the pot. They just gave all the employees a pass to a steak dinner in the lodge Dining Room. Tomorrow night, Rob and I are going to the Dining Room, and they're going to cook my trout that I caught in the lake. They filet it for you and serve it with a roll, salad, baked potato, and vegetables for $1.50. What a deal!

That's what everybody who catches anything does with them. The biggest one I caught was 18 inches. We have a sign on the dock that says mine is the biggest one caught this summer. A lot of people come down the Cleetwood Trail to the boat dock to fish. I went to Klamath Falls and bought a bunch of lures for 19 cents each and sold them at the boat shack for $1.50 each. That's the name of the game. Screw the touri. I'm so sick of looking at campers, trailers, and motorhomes. I'm going to start taking pics. We can get free disposable cameras. I now have $416 in my bank account. Tell Mike and the rest of the boys 'hi.' Hope you all have a good summer.

In another letter, P.T. wrote,

Good to hear from you boys. Wish you were having a better summer, but with Neil and all that's happened, I understand. But summers are the time to groove, so keep your spirits up. I am.

Guess who came up and stayed with us? Randy! We had a hell of a time. He just left yesterday. I was just taking my clothes off for a shower when Chaz laid your letter on me. He got my mail for me tonight. Anyway, I was going to take a fast shower and get my butt up to the lodge. There's a double-kegger, and I plan on getting wasted.

I'm glad to hear you beat the older guys in softball. We should have beaten them the first time, but too many errors. Good old Lu'. You can always depend on him to have his act together when it comes to Mike slapping him in the face. I'm afraid that if that would have been me, Mike would have had to pick up his face off the floor, but you know how that goes.

I wish that Mike would grow up and straighten out a little. He's got some kind of problem other than the junkies. Mom called me, and said Mike climbed all over her case. He told her she didn't care, and if that dumbshit only knew. Sometimes, I think he's growing up, and the next minute, he'll act like a baby. I've said it a thousand times: "The only one who can do anything for Mike is Mike." It's got to come from within, so I guess there's no use talking about it.

I just finished *Bury My Heart at Wounded Knee*, and if you want to read a really good book, read that one. By the time you finish it, you're so frustrated and depressed that you feel like going out and telling them "you can live with me." I'll be coming home on September 1, so I'll see you boys then.

P.T.

Birdie's time on Division Street lasted about a month before Lu' moved to Los Angeles, and Birdie, who had received a temporary reprieve from the military for the marijuana bust, decided it was time to leave Portland for a while. Instead of Canada, he bolted to California and, ultimately, Mexico. His traveling companion as far as the San Francisco Bay Area was Craig Kubiak.

Birdie's latest Volkswagen Bug was in sorry shape, like all of his previous vehicles, but time was running out. Any number of threats were looming: his dad, the police, the Selective Service, and possibly others who knew where the family home was located. On more than one occasion, Birdie's younger brother Doug heard the doorbell and answered the door to find a police officer. His typical response was, "We don't know where Birdie is."

Heading south toward Berkeley and San Diego, Birdie and Craig drove through the Avenue of the Giants and continued down Highway 1 along the California coastline to San Francisco. The Volkswagen did fine down that stretch of highway, and after a night at a state park near Mendocino, they rolled across the Golden Gate Bridge with "Mrs. Robinson" playing at full volume, straight out of a scene from *The Graduate*.

Hyde Street Pier in San Francisco

In the fifties, Birdie, Emile, and his mom and dad had traveled to the Bay Area to see his dad's sister, Mace McInnes. When they visited her home in Redwood City, it usually meant a trip to San Francisco and Sacramento. Mace had married Bill Freeman, and the Freemans—Mace, Bill, and their children, Caren and Laurie—hosted Birdie's family. The environment always seemed tense, mostly because of Mace. The family had a third child that the family never acknowledged. Birdie learned later that the child was institutionalized because of mental or physical disabilities.

Birdie and Craig arrived at the residence of Tom Moriarity, Lu's older brother, and his wife, Sarah, on Parker Street, a few blocks from the campus of the University of California, Berkeley. They rendezvoused with Chuck Schneider, and the trio bunked at Tom's for about three weeks, much longer than intended because they all contracted a gastrointestinal illness. They recovered while watching the 1972 Olympics, the most memorable match being the much-anticipated men's basketball final, possibly the most controversial event in Olympic history resulting in the first loss for Team USA since the Olympic sport began.

The Olympics featured the usual diving and gymnastics, track and field, and other athletic endeavors, but basketball was captivating to the sickly group. In previous Olympics, the United States had won seven gold medals, and the current team was favored to win another in Munich. The United States convincingly won its first eight games of the tournament, advancing its overall Olympic record to 63-0 and setting up the final against the Soviet Union.

The US team would be the youngest in history. American college players usually participated in the Olympics before turning professional, so the US team always had new players every four years. The 1972 team did not have a clear leader. A rising star, Bill Walton, declined an invitation to participate. Nevertheless, the team was the favorite featuring such players as Doug Collins and Tommy Burleson. The basketball gold medal was the last event in the Olympics to be contested. The Soviets were already in command of the overall medal standings.

The Soviets surprised the Americans early in the game and led at halftime 26-21. The United States regained the lead toward the end, but a major controversy would follow. After Collins' second free throw put the United States ahead, the refs ruled that time should be added on the clock. Following three inbounds plays, the Soviets scored the winning points. The United States ultimately refused to accept the silver medals the country had been awarded because of the disputed outcome. It was an ignominious ending indeed.

When the boys recovered from their ailment, they explored San Francisco for a few days. The sights spanned the entire San Francisco Peninsula including Fisherman's Wharf, the Presidio, Golden Gate Park, and the Cliff House, preserved in the Golden Gate National Recreation Area. The Cliff House, a small restaurant, had been part of a much larger operation associated with the Sutro Baths, a large, privately owned public saltwater swimming pool complex in the Land's End area of the Bay Area.

Having consumed blue bellybutton acid, they jumped the caution tape near the Cliff House to examine the ruins of the bath house and explore the myriad tunnels into the bowels of the old facility. Destroyed by fire in 1966 while being demolished, all that remained were the foundations of the pools, blocked off stairs and passageways, and a tunnel with a deep crevice leading to the ocean. As they wandered through the caves, bats suddenly appeared.

"What was that?" asked Birdie.

"Bats!" cried Chuck. "Let's get the hell out of here."

They spent the rest of the evening in Golden Gate Park until the effects of the drug subsided, eventually stopping at a Jack in the Box, a fast-food restaurant, for a couple of burgers. The chain, established in 1951, was unique because it featured a drive-up window, the first of its kind. As Birdie approached the speaker box, he clipped the clown head off its stand with his side view mirror. Hastily, they placed their order and split, fleeing to Berkeley without incident.

Birdie always had a bad feeling about Leap Years, and 1972 would be no different. He was born in a leap year, 1952, and struggled for the first few months. In Italy and throughout the Mediterranean, leap year is considered an omen of bad luck. In fact, a uniquely Italian saying notes, "Anno biseto, anno funesto," meaning "leap year, gloomy year." In other words, bad luck.

Now he was on the run from the military with his companions, and Nixon would soon be reelected, much to the chagrin of many. The headlines of the day bore that assumption out: Vietnam Conflict Continues, Polio Runs Rampant, US Detonates First Hydrogen Bomb, Violent Protests in Egypt.

CHAPTER FOUR

Manic Migration

Fall 1972: After about three weeks at Tom's, Birdie proceeded south. Now traveling solo, he stopped in Monterey and Santa Cruz and then continued down through Big Sur, visiting Hearst Castle, built by newspaper baron William Randolph Hearst. His Volkswagen Bug wasn't running well, but it wasn't yet dead. The spark plugs continually clogged with carbon resin, requiring an occasional stop to remove the residue with a wire brush. Birdie cruised through LA without stopping and pressed on to San Diego, where he bunked with childhood friends living in Ocean Beach.

After a week in San Diego, he called his mom for an update on his status with the Selective Service System. She said she had been "worried to death" about Birdie and asked if he was okay. She said he had received his Notice of Classification and that he was 1-A, meaning "eligible for induction into the armed services." She said that he had three months to report after the marijuana charge could be resolved in court, effectively delaying his induction into the army. *I still have time before reporting,* he thought.

Knowing he had some breathing room, Birdie crossed the border into Tijuana, a border town with millions of residents. He met a couple of Mexican girls, sisters, at a bar, and after a bit of small talk, they complimented his understanding of Spanish. Seemingly enamored with the American, they invited him into their home. Smoking dope and drinking Tecate, the girls grew even more amorous, luring him into the bedroom for a bout of lovemaking. Shortly afterward, when their parents came home abruptly, Birdie had to make a hasty exit out the back door. He quickly hopped into his car and proceeded south to Mazatlán.

The car still ran roughly, but every so often, he pulled over and cleaned the carbon off the spark plugs. Just as he arrived in Mazatlán, the Volkswagen finally and emphatically gave up. Desperate for money to fix the car, Birdie applied for a job at *The Mazatlán Post*, the local newspaper. Because of his knowledge of Spanish and experience as a novice journalist, the editor hired him to cover sports and work as a general assignment reporter.

Most of his assignments focused on baseball and soccer, two favorite pastimes in Mexico. After a few weeks of reporting on sports and hard news, his editor asked him to cover a bullfight in town. Birdie seemed game, but on the assignment covering a bullfight at the Plaza de Toros, he discovered it wasn't at all what he expected. Bullfighting was still a large part of the culture of Mazatlán and all of Mexico. The event followed a particular sequence: the entrance of the bull, the picador, the banderilleros and other celebrants, and finally the matador. During the halftime, those in attendance witnessed the Mazatlán Dancing Horses.

In the end, the matador killed the bull. Birdie watched as the poor creature writhed in agony, and he cringed. For what purpose? Sport? Entertainment? The sheer cruelty of the finish was more than he could handle, and the revulsion would linger for a long time. Later that day, he submitted his story and tendered his resignation from the newspaper.

After collecting his last paycheck, and with his Beetle running again, Birdie pointed north for the US border. Entering Mexico was one thing, but leaving was a different matter. He had no problem passing through the Mexican checkpoint, but the American checkpoint was more complicated. Border guards waved him over and then rifled through the car, finding a resinous pipe used for smoking marijuana.

The guard asked him to step out of the car, and he was escorted to a modular facility nearby. He was frisked and asked to strip naked. Once bare, two surly border guards conducted an anal cavity search, mining for drugs. Once deemed clean, Birdie was dismissed to his Beetle, where he found his belongings scattered on the ground. Even the headlights had been yanked from their sockets, and he had to reinstall them. Shaken but relieved, he hit the road to San Diego, arriving at his friend's flat in Ocean Beach. He promptly called his mom, but she had bad news.

"We received an Order to Report for Armed Forces Examination, and under special notes, it says, 'If you fail to report for or submit to an examination, reexamination, or to comply with other instructions contained, you will be ordered to report for induction.'"

"Well, I guess it's time to come home," said Birdie.

"I'm on my way then. See you in about a week."

The journey, however, would take a bit longer because of several detours along the way. His first would be Disneyland. Birdie had always wanted to visit the "happiest place on earth."

The McInnes brood was introduced to the wide world of Walt Disney as children. Their mom loved all things Disney dating back to her youth, when brothers Walt and Roy founded the Disney Brothers Cartoon Studio and introduced animated characters like Mickey Mouse, Donald Duck, and many others. The kids watched cartoons on Saturday morning while consuming bowls of cereal. On television, Disney introduced *The Mickey Mouse Club*, an American variety show that aired on ABC from 1955–1959. The program featured a regular but ever-changing cast of mostly preteen and teen performers. The character of Mickey Mouse appeared on every show in vintage cartoons created for theatrical release and shorts. In all the cartoons, Mickey Mouse was voiced by Walt Disney himself.

    The show was hosted by an adult, Jimmie Dodd, a songwriter and the Head Mouseketeer. He provided leadership for the young Mouseketeers on and off the show. In addition to his other contributions, he often provided short segments that encouraged young viewers to make the right moral choices. Roy Williams, a staff artist at Disney, appeared in the show as Jimmy's sidekick—known to viewers as The Big Mouseketeer. He was the one who suggested that cast members should wear Mickey and Minnie Mouse ears.

    Birdie was particularly enamored by one specific Mouseketeer, Annette Funicello, an attractive young woman of Italian American heritage. She would later star in teenage beach movies and other films and television. When Disneyland opened on July 17, 1955, Birdie and Emile longed to travel there. Mom suggested a road trip to California, since the McInnes family had cousins in Redwood City, followed by a trip to Disneyland. The idea seemed feasible. Dad, however, refused to incur such an expense. Hence, they never went, much to everyone's disappointment.

En route to Portland, Birdie stopped at Disneyland, enjoying every minute of it, especially the Pirates of the Caribbean ride. After several days there (he slept in a sleeping bag in his Bug in the massive Disneyland parking lot), he escaped from LA. Halfway up the Grapevine, the long stretch of windy mountain highway connecting the Los Angeles basin to the San Joaquin Valley to the north, the Bug started to fail again. At the top, he pulled over and cleaned the spark plugs well enough to make it off the mountain. At the bottom of the Grapevine, however, the Bug died, this time for good. He called his mom and explained his dilemma, asking her to wire money for a new engine. Fortunately, she relented. He called a tow truck to drag the Bug into Bakersfield. When he found a mechanic who seemed to offer reasonable prices, he authorized the purchase of a short block engine.

"How long will it take?" he asked the owner.

"About two days" came the reply.

"What will I do in the meantime?" asked Birdie.

"Whatever you want, but come back in two days."

It was blazing hot in Bakersfield, and he took refuge in a local city park. It was 114 degrees Fahrenheit, and he tried to stay in the shade. The park appeared to be a hangout for numerous down-on-their-luck types, so he kept close watch on his meager belongings. As the heat grew more intense, a book of matches ignited in his pocket. Surprised, he burned his hand pulling them out. He slept when he could, but the park denizens were creeping too close for comfort. He only dozed briefly for the most part.

Finally, the mechanic returned, and Birdie begged him to let him stay in the shop until the work was done. The mechanic agreed, and while driving Birdie back to his shop, he conducted a scenic tour through Bakersfield, pointing out the elaborate residences of Merle Haggard and Buck Owens. "Bakersfield is known as Nashville West, you know."

"I did not know that," said Birdie.

"I have a surprise for you," added the mechanic. "We've put a Porsche engine in your Volkswagen."

"What?" Birdie gasped, anticipating a bill he could not pay. "I only have $400 to work with."

"Don't worry. It won't cost you any more than the original estimate, but you'll have a much stronger engine."

"Great!"

Testing the rebuilt Porsche engine, Birdie could hardly believe how the Bug had been transformed. He could pop a wheelie if he punched it but didn't dare because the tires were so poor, and he would need them to get back to Portland. Saying goodbye to the mechanic, Birdie continued his journey back home. He stopped in Berkeley for a bit of rest and repose at Tom and Sue's place and visited his aunt, his dad's sister, in Redwood City. Aunt Mace left Portland after high school to attend Stanford University at her father's expense. She was bright in high school, and her grades merited admission to such a prestigious university, but comparatively speaking, she was marginal at best among the brilliance of many at the private university.

Mace greeted Birdie with a look of disgust; his shoulder-length hair was disheveled from his long, arduous road trip. Birdie's cousins were pleasant enough, but the older one resembled her mother in temperament. The family had a ping-pong table in their basement, so the kids went downstairs for a couple of matches. After two quick games, the girls gave up, and they all went upstairs for lunch.

"What are you going to do with your life?' asked Aunt Mace.

"My strong suit is writing, so I plan to major in journalism," replied Birdie.

"Well, that's nice," she replied, rolling her eyes.

Birdie then bade farewell and proceeded up the peninsula to Berkeley. After a few more days at Tom and Sue's, he placed one final call to his mom. "You'd better get here muy pronto, or they will be coming after you," she said.

"I'm on my way, Mom. See you tomorrow."

Arriving in Portland, Birdie read the note from the Selective Service and called to inquire. "Yes, we'd like to see you right away," the official said. "Now that your marijuana charge has been cleared, we'd like to reevaluate you."

At that point, P.T. was back in Portland, and the two met to discuss their respective futures. "I'm screwed," Birdie said with resignation.

P.T. then suggested something completely different. "Hey, why don't we join the army, and then you won't have to get drafted."

"Join the army? What do you mean *we*?" Birdie asked. "Isn't that like jumping from the frying pan into the fire?"

"No, listen. You're going to be drafted anyway, right? Why don't we join together and serve in Germany or someplace even safer, like stateside?"

"I don't know, P.T."

The more they discussed P.T.'s suggestion, the more Birdie liked the idea. They often drove to a point east of Mt. Hood Community College, observed the barges moving up the Columbia River, and talked. Finally, Birdie said, "I'm in."

While visiting an army recruiter at Mall 205, they announced their intentions to enlist. The recruiter was delighted. "Not too many fish just jump into the boat," he said with a smile. "Why do you fellows want to join?"

Birdie muttered something about "drafted anyway," and P.T. noted he wanted to see Europe and the rest of the world.

"Well, I think we can fix you boys up. We'll schedule a time to show up at the armed forces testing center in downtown Portland for physical and psychological testing."

The next week, they drove downtown for a full evaluation. Everything went smoothly, and they received notice that they soon would depart for basic training at Fort Ord in Northern California.

Friends and family scheduled a farewell party for the two inductees held at P.T. and Lu's residence on Division Street. The hoedown became a party to end all parties. However, their buddy, Vin Beasley, recently discharged from the army, was adamant that they abandon the idea of joining the army. "Don't do it," Vin said emphatically.

"What am I going to do, Vin?" asked Birdie. "I'll be drafted next month anyway!"

"Whatever you envision about the army, it will be a hundred times worse. Trust me, don't do it."

The more the drinking continued, the more morose Birdie became. He struggled back to his apartment at 2:00 a.m., sleeping restlessly until he rolled out of bed at 7:00 a.m. to report for induction. It was a mighty struggle, but they drove downtown, and their collective mood was morose. No one said a word. After parking the vehicle, the pair reported to the front desk. "You two take a seat over in the waiting area, and we'll get to you shortly," said the desk sergeant.

It was a depressing scene, so Birdie curled up on a bench seat and fell asleep. Meanwhile, P.T. called his girlfriend, Gina, one call after the other. Birdie noticed something odd was happening. "Gina has talked me out of it," P.T. suddenly blurted.

"What?" Birdie gasped. A collective sense of relief, anticipation, and anxiety swept over the pair. "What the hell are we going to do?" he whispered.

"Let's get out of here," said P.T.

Sashaying past the front desk and walking out into the open air of downtown Portland, they felt exhilarated. Hopping in Birdie's VW Bug, they sped across the Morrison Bridge to Vin's place to break the news.

"Best move you boys have ever made," said Vin.

"Where shall we go?" asked Birdie.

"They'll be looking for us, and people are driving to the airport to say goodbye. Let's go to Rockaway Beach until this whole thing blows over," said P.T. It was one of his favorite escapes. "After all, we didn't sign any papers committing us to join the army."

P.T. was correct; the beach was a great place to seek solace and refuge, and they hadn't made an official commitment to join. A host of friends and relatives showed up at the airport to see the boys off. When P.T.'s older brother, Harry, asked where they were, the man in charge said, "Well, they must have eloped, because they're not here." That was that.

Birdie was still subject to the draft. By the end of December, Nixon had been reelected, and the Vietnam war continued. Birdie's twentieth birthday came and went.

P.T., Birdie, and Lu', though intelligent, had never historically scored well in terms of deportment. They typically performed poorly in the behavioral areas such as "respect for authority," "cooperation and dependability," "application," and "perseverance." Enrolled at Mt. Hood Community College for the winter term, they spent their spare time pursuing the usual shenanigans. They enjoyed driving to the Portland International Airport, lying on the edge of the runway, and watching the Boeing 707s pass about a hundred feet over their heads while landing. Adrenaline junkies.

Otherwise, December was mostly depressing for Birdie but not without significance. Apollo 17 blasted off on the last manned mission and landed on the moon on Birdie's birthday, December 11. Roberto Clemente died tragically in a plane crash while on a goodwill mission to the Caribbean, and President Harry Truman passed away. Times were becoming increasingly tense and bleak. North Vietnamese negotiators walked out of the Paris Peace Accords during Nixon's Christmas bombing of Vietnam.

Birdie and Lu' focused on lower division basics like literature and science while delving into the journalism curriculum with a Mass Media and Society class. Then, in late January, an Associated Press report announced, "Draft calls eliminated by US," and a kicker read, "Volunteer force grows." Birdie could hardly believe his eyes as he scanned the story:

> WASHINGTON (AP)—Secretary of Defense Melvin R. Laird announced that "the use of the draft has ended." His action, placing the nation's armed forces on an all-volunteer footing for the first time in nearly 25 years, came five months ahead of President Nixon's goal.

In a message to senior defense officials, Laird said: "With the signing of the peace agreement in Paris today, and after receiving a report from the Secretary of the Army that he foresees no need for further inductions, I wish to inform you that the armed forces henceforth will depend exclusively on volunteer soldiers, sailors, airmen and Marines." Laird's decision cancels plans to draft about 5,000 men before June, 1973, when legal authority to draft young men into the armed forces will expire. Pentagon officials said the flow of volunteers, spurred by a series of military pay raises and improved fringe benefits, has encouraged them to believe these 5,000 men can be raised through recruiting. Although the authority to draft young men into the military service will die June 30, the Selective Service law will remain on the books so that the stand-by machinery can be revived, if necessary.

To use that machinery, a president would have to go back to Congress and ask for restoration of the induction authority. Young men still will be required to register for the draft at age 18. The Pentagon has been moving toward an all-volunteer force for the past four years, as it has gradually withdrawn US forces from Vietnam and, parallel to that, reduced the size of US forces worldwide. The Vietnam War peak in inductions came in 1968, when 383,626 young men were drafted. Last year, the number of inductions was down to 48,000. As a practical matter, nobody has been drafted into the Army since early last month. Laird announced the end of the draft only a few days before he is due to hand over his post to Elliot L. Richardson.

Needless to say, Birdie was elated. Reclassified as I-H, he would now legally avoid military service. He enthusiastically delved further into his studies and got his academic groove back. Taking classes and hanging with his homies, he particularly enjoyed his journalism and literature classes. In February, a recruiter from Crater Lake Lodge visited the Mt. Hood campus. Since P.T., a veteran of Crater Lake Lodge, would be coming back for a second season, Birdie thought, *What the hell. I might as well apply.*

CHAPTER FIVE
New Day Dawning

Winter 1973: Birdie signed up for a Crater Lake interview, and it went very well. The recruiter asked, "What positions might you be interested in applying for, Mr. McInnes?"

"Probably the boat mechanic position," Birdie replied.

"What are your qualifications?"

"I worked on a charter boat down in Depot Bay, so I learned how to drive a watercraft. I have worked on my own cars with my dad, so I know something about mechanics."

"Okay" came the reply. "We'll let you know if we want to follow up with you in the near future."

A few weeks later, Birdie's brother, Doug, received a phone call from a Mr. Fisher, and he passed along a message to Birdie, who was at his parents' house doing his laundry.

"Who is Mr. Fisher?" asked Birdie. "Not a cop, I hope."

"No, he said he was from Crater Lake."

"What? Did you get his number?"

"Yes," replied Doug.

Birdie practically leapt for the phone. A few moments later, he was talking with Mr. Fisher.

"It says here on your application that you've applied for the boat mechanic spot," said Mr. Fisher.

"Yes, that would be my first choice, but I'm open to other positions."

"We already have a boat mechanic, but we have an opening for a tour guide and boat operator."

"That sounds great. What would it require?"

"You'll have to pass a coast guard boat operator's test and learn about the lake. Do you have experience working on a boat?"

"Yes, actually. I was a bait boy on a charter fishing boat at the Oregon coast."

"Okay. We'll send you the paperwork with all the requirements in a few days."

"Great!"

He then received two letters from Crater Lake Lodge. The first one read, "To Birdie McInnes: You have been selected to work at Crater Lake Lodge this summer as a member of the boat crew. If you want this job, read the enclosed contract, and mail it back immediately. If you do not want the job, please mail back the contract in the enclosed envelope unsigned so that we may offer the job to someone else. This job will be held for you for ten days from the date of this mailing."

Birdie signed the contract and mailed it immediately. The next letter, more cordial and friendly, read, "Dear Mr. McInnes, I am enclosing a copy of *Crater Lake: The Story of Its Origin* by Howel Williams. Please read this book before you arrive, as it will cover many questions which you will be asked this summer by tourists. I am also enclosing a copy of sample questions that may appear on the coast guard launch operator's test you must pass before you become a tour guide. I would recommend that you read *Piloting Seamanship and Small Boat Handling* by Chapman, which can be picked up at almost any library. If you have any questions, please contact Ron Jackson, whose phone number is provided in this letter. He will be your direct supervisor. Sincerely, Mr. Fisher."

Birdie was overjoyed. He couldn't wait to call P.T. "That's great!" said P.T. "When do you take the test?"
"Soon."

The United States Coast Guard Limited Masters License required that all launch operators participate in a two-day training followed by a test. The license would be valid for five years. He studied hard in class and easily passed the test. Meanwhile, Birdie and Lu' loved the science classes they took together at Mt. Hood Community College, particularly geology. The class focused on the Columbia River Gorge and the layering that had occurred for millennia, precipitated by the Missoula floods, cataclysmic glacial lake outbursts that swept periodically across the plains of Eastern Washington. The floods formed massive coulees along the Columbia River.

They took numerous field trips up the Columbia Gorge, where the professor could illustrate his lectures and enhance their learning. The great floods swept up the Willamette Basin farther downstream and westward toward the Pacific Ocean. Meanwhile, Birdie read the Williams book on the geology of Crater Lake to understand the unique features of the caldera and learned a lot about Oregon's only national park. Millennia before the establishment of the park—long before the existence of a lake for that matter—there was a mountain, and what a mountain it was. More than four hundred thousand years ago, Mt. Mazama began its building process with cracks in the earth's crust, signaling the rise of a great new stratovolcano in southern Oregon.

"In time, a vast magma chamber supplied most of the raw material for the building of Mt. Mazama," wrote Williams, the University of California, Berkeley professor and geologist who authored the definitive tome of the region. "Increasingly, violent surges from below piled volumes of molten rock, ash and pumice on the surface. Eventually, periods of cooling and hardening alternated with episodes of eruption. After more than a million years, Mt. Mazama had risen to a height of more than 12,000 feet above sea level, towering far above its neighbors," Williams wrote. "In the whole length of the Cascade Range, there were few volcanoes that rivaled it in size" (Williams, Howel. *Crater Lake: The Story of Its Origin*. Berkeley: University of California Press, 1970).

Eventually, wrote Williams, the mountain moved into a cataclysmic period of eruption, and volcanic ash and dust storms would envelope the peak and blacken the sun. The Klamath and Modoc native peoples of the marshes below knew the mountain only by sound and the trembling at their feet. Finally, the pace of events quickened. Without warning, Mt. Mazama released a giant, billowing cloud of black smoke—punctuated with bursts of lightning—high into the atmosphere. Avalanches of hot ash sped down mountain valleys, incinerating everything in their path. Lethal gas fumes engulfed native villages in the marshes. As the activity grew in strength, winds veered toward the northeast and carried smoke and ash as far away as Montana, Alberta, and Saskatchewan.

The next time the people of the marsh could gaze toward the mountain—to their surprise and astonishment—the top half of the peak had vanished. More than five thousand feet of mountain had disappeared. Today, geologists concur that the summit of Mt. Mazama collapsed within itself when a pool of magma inside the mountain drained or was expelled as ash, creating a huge cavity. In short, the mountain could no longer support its own weight. Williams' book also covered the native myths of Crater Lake. Mythic battles between Llao (Mt. Mazama) and Skell (Mt. Shasta)—like many great folktales from other lands—are based on fact.

Birdie was fascinated by the assigned readings about Crater Lake.

The lake is the deepest in the United States and the seventh deepest in the world. The newly formed caldera took thousands of years to fill with water after Mt. Mazama collapsed. Today, the elevation at lake level is 6,178 feet above sea level with the surrounding caldera walls ascending several thousand feet above the level of the lake. Mt. Scott, a parasitic cone near the rim of the caldera, stands at nearly nine thousand feet above sea level.

The features on the caldera wall are stunning and varied, with creative names like Pumice Castle, the Wineglass, Chaski Slide, and Devil's Backbone. Crater Lake features two islands, Phantom Ship and Wizard Island, a cinder cone resembling a wizard's hat on the surface of the lake. Its greatest depth is 1,932 feet. Another small cinder cone known as Merriam Cone came close but failed to make it to the surface level of the lake. The bowl of the caldera provides no inlets or outlets to Crater Lake, so the actual level of the lake stays fairly constant due to a balance of annual precipitation and constant evaporation. Another unique feature is the "Old Man in the Lake," a petrified hemlock that has floated around the lake vertically for perhaps hundreds of years.

Another book, *Along Crater Lake Roads* by George C. Ruhle, provided information so that the boat crew could identify the flora and fauna in the park. Although the mean elevation within the park is about 5,500 feet above sea level, the natural environment is still quite diverse. Mammals exist in abundance, of course, the most common being golden-mantled ground squirrels, black bears, deer, coyote, porcupines, and Roosevelt elk. Deciduous trees include thin leaf alder, quaking aspen, and black cottonwood, while conifers consist of Douglas fir, Shasta red fir, subalpine fir, white fir, Western hemlock, mountain hemlock, lodgepole pine, ponderosa pine, sugar pine, Western white pine, white bark pine, and Engelmann spruce. In an odd coincidence, the Phantom Ship, a relatively small rock island, features every type of conifer found in the park (Ruhle, George C. *Along Crater Lake Roads: A Road Guide to Crater Lake National Park Oregon*. Crater Lake National Park, OR: 1964).

Birdie had come to believe that the paradox of life moves in cycles, undulating between the yin and the yang, from low points to high points with constant movement in between. Just six months before, he was doomed to life the US Army. Paradox had seemingly become a constant theme in his life, that sense of swinging between two poles. So much in his life seemed to be either/or: life or death, day or night, hot or cold. He knew he had mood swings but not to the point of being bipolar. He did, however, acknowledge suffering from obsessive-compulsive disorder. He rarely sat still and needed constant activity in his waking hours. *What is the nature of our lives*? he would ponder. *How is such behavior explained? Is it heredity, or are we a product of our environment?* He wasn't sure.

Many of his mates seemed to be free spirits whose souls had been trampled by the priests, nuns, and lay teachers who had constantly harassed and harangued them. Some had it coming. Some did not. It all seemed so arbitrary to Birdie. As a result of the draconian environment at OLPS, many were doomed to fail, yet others exceeded expectations. Another paradox. Birdie puzzled about such issues as he prepared to leave home for Crater Lake. He would miss his family, but there would be no turning back.

CHAPTER SIX

Mobilizing a Transition

Spring 1973: With grades posted for winter quarter, Birdie felt upbeat and optimistic, a far cry from only six months before. He was pursuing his college career and had a dream job for the summer at one of the seven natural wonders of the world. Now it would be a matter of funding this unlikely enterprise known as "higher education" by working summers to achieve his goal of a degree in journalism.

The next letter he received from Crater Lake Lodge summarized general information for his new job.

> Over 150 of the highest type of young people are employed here for the season, and definite positions in some cases cannot be assigned until after arrival. Rules and regulations are at a minimum, but STRICT OBSERVANCE is required. If you feel you cannot conform to the rules or work at any job assigned to you, please return your contract unsigned, so we can select an alternate with as little delay as possible.
>
> Our operation is short term, business is hectic, and every employee hired is needed full time in his

or her job. It is up to you to see that you eat properly, get enough rest, etc., so that you will not put fellow employees "on the spot" by having to take time off work, resulting in inadequate staff. Beer or other alcoholic beverages (or depressants, stimulants, or hallucinogenic drugs, unless on authorized prescription) are not permitted on the premises, and anyone found in possession of any of these will be discharged. Employees will not be relieved from duty during the summer to attend weddings or other events except for those of an emergency nature unless agreed to prior to employment.

A charge of $3.55 per day is deducted from your salary for room and board. All employees eat in the cafeteria and live in the dormitories, either in the lodge or near the service station at park headquarters. Dorm rooms accommodate four to six people; space is limited; an extensive wardrobe will cause storage problems as well as being unnecessary. All bedding is furnished, but towels must be supplied by each employee. Housemothers will supervise the dormitories to prevent excessive noise or conduct that would disturb guests with rooms nearby. Closing hours are enforced for this reason.

A $50 deposit is required to ensure that you will fulfill your part of the contract and to cover breakage or loss of badges, keys, bedding, etc. for which you are responsible. At the satisfactory conclusion of your commitment, the $50 will be returned to you PLUS A BONUS of $50. If you terminate employment prematurely for good reasons beyond your control, and with our permission, your $50 will be refunded. Facilities for washing clothes are provided in the basement of the lodge at no cost, though use of the dryer is ten cents. Employees put on a program for guests every evening from 8:30–9:00 p.m. These programs consist of music, dancing, skits, etc.

Overnight leaves are limited to three times per season, and permission must be obtained in all cases from management. In addition, for employees under the age of twenty-one, their parents' or guardians' written consent is required, and this must be presented at the time of signing your contract. All employees must sign out when leaving the area, giving destination and expected time of return. This is a safeguard for the employee as well as enabling management to intelligently answer questions in the event of a long-distance phone call. If you drive (at your own expense), your car must be registered with the National Park Service and bear a sticker showing that you are legally in the park. In any event, your transportation to the park is your responsibility. If requested, transportation will be provided from Klamath Falls to Crater Lake at a predetermined time as specified in your contract.

About two weeks before his departure to Crater Lake, Birdie lost the only key to his VW. Panicked, he asked P.T. for advice. "I have a buddy who can set you up," P.T. replied.

Birdie paid a visit to the Union 76 station on N.E. Sixtieth and Glisan to talk to Keith Harrington.

"Yeah, I can install a toggle switch." said Harrington. "It will allow you to turn on the ignition, but it won't turn the engine over. You'll have to compression-start the car with the toggle switch on. Make sure you always park on a hill, which will make it a lot easier."

"Sounds good," replied Birdie. "Thank you."

Much to his delight, the concept worked. VWs didn't weigh that much, so even if he found himself on a flat, it would simply be a matter of push-starting the car.

The next week, Birdie and P.T. served as ushers at a friend's wedding. Jim Wexler, a childhood buddy from OLPS, would wed Jan Boykin, his high school sweetheart. Their wedding plan was elaborate. The wedding party was fitted at a posh rental facility downtown; groomsmen wore suits of purple paisley—the fashion of the day—and the women wore white dresses. Before the ceremony, the party posed for pictures. Birdie had parked on the hill outside the church so he could compression-start the vehicle afterward. He parked the Bug to the curb with wheels turned inward and set the brake, but with no key, he couldn't lock the door. During the photo session, Gina rushed into the church, after having a smoke outside, with a frantic look on her face. She mouthed the words several times so Birdie could see. "Your car has rolled down the hill!"

Birdie eventually understood her and excused himself to look outside. His car had indeed rolled down the hill, stopping when it collided with a small sapling directly across the street from the church vestibule. "Oh, man!" he muttered. "Some punk prank, no doubt."

The front hood was dented, but otherwise, the Bug survived, and it was still in position to compression-start. Birdie returned, and the photo session continued.

Life with Birdie's dad wasn't all bad. For example, he had a penchant for outdoor activities. Many of the students at OLPS were in the Boy Scouts, and his dad helped with carpooling to activities and campouts. He knew that Birdie and his siblings loved outdoor activities in the Pacific Northwest. As a mountaineer, his dad was a member of the Mazamas, a climbing club based in Portland that led numerous student climbing expeditions. When Birdie was eleven, he climbed Mt. Hood with the group, followed by Mt. St. Helens the next season. Emile and Doug also climbed those peaks with their dad, and the whole family enjoyed camping and fishing in the national forests near Portland.

The Hogsback near the summit of Mt. Hood

On campouts, Birdie particularly loved the ritual of campfires. He spent long periods of time staring into a campfire, devoting his attention to the flames. He found it a deeply meditative, inspiring, and enlightening experience. Since ancient times, fire has been a symbol of creativity and passion, fueling artists, writers, and musicians for centuries. Campfires had a way of keeping Birdie's mind in the present in a meditative experience. He loved the scent of a campfire and the smell of wood burning sharp and earthy, providing a wonderfully Zen experience. Paradoxically, fire has the power to create and destroy.

As Birdie progressed through the Boys Scouts, the troop enjoyed campouts once a month, even in the winter. Troop 138 rented Catholic Youth Organization facilities like Camp Howard and Camp Barton outside the city near the Mt. Hood National Forest. During the summers, the troop would spend a week at a time at more elaborate camps like Camp Meriwether on the Oregon coast, Camp Baldwin on the east side of Mt. Hood near Dufur, Oregon, and Camp Spirit Lake at the foot of Mt. St. Helens in Washington. Troop 138 even undertook an epic trip to Yellowstone National Park one summer, with stops at Farewell Bend State Park on the Snake River, Craters of Moon National Monument, Lewis and Clark Caverns in Montana, and Liberty Lake near Spokane, Washington. They bunked at air force and army bases and at US Forest Service or National Park Service campgrounds along the way.

Aside from Boy Scouts, Birdie and his family camped at Forest Service campgrounds in the Mt. Hood National Forest. On extended trips, they camped at state parks on the Oregon Coast and at Diamond Lake near Crater Lake. On at least two trips to Diamond Lake, the family attempted to visit Crater Lake. In both instances, however, the lake was obscured by fog, so they never got to actually "see" it. Instead, the siblings passed the time at Diamond Lake, swatting mosquitoes and otherwise making life miserable for their dad. In one instance, they were roasting marshmallows around the campfire when one marshmallow caught fire. Alarmed, Doug flicked it toward the fire. Instead, it landed directly on Dad's new White Stag windbreaker.

Everyone laughed, which didn't enhance his dad's cool. He was livid. The siblings believed Doug was doomed to suffer the "wrath of Dad." Fortunately, Doug survived, but that would mark the end of campouts at Diamond Lake. Hence, Birdie never had the opportunity to visit Crater Lake, so the only images in his mind were those he saw in picture books and postcards. Now he would not only see Crater Lake but also work at the park as a tour guide and boat operator for the summer.

With P.T. in Phoenix, Birdie enjoyed life away from home rent free while attending Mt. Hood Community College. He even had a bedroom to himself. The subjects that term were general requirement classes, and Birdie and Lu' continued with their studies while otherwise enjoying life with the boys and, especially, the girls. One night, an old girlfriend, Sharon Roberts, asked to come home with him after a long stint at The Bucket, a popular tavern in midtown Portland where Lu' tended bar.

When they arrived, Birdie had a sense of what was coming. "You remember that 'four-dot' Oly label I signed for you?" Sharon asked.

"Well, uh, yes!" said Birdie, anticipating her next line.

"Well, I'm here to cash it in."

"Oh boy!" He knew what that meant: a night of passion with Sharon, who would remain a good friend for life, unlike many of Birdie's other girlfriends.

As spring quarter concluded, Birdie moved his belongings to his gramma's basement for storage. Lu' was preparing for new digs with some of the other boys at Foul House II in Northeast Portland, and P.T. would meet Birdie at Crater Lake. At the end of the quarter, Birdie learned his report card was excellent, much to his mom's delight. Now it was a matter of packing the essentials he would need for the summer and saying his goodbyes.

CHAPTER SEVEN

Dream Season

Summer 1973: Birdie's new gig wasn't the only news of the day. Though President Nixon had been reelected the previous November, he was in big trouble by summer. The Watergate scandal unfolded with televised hearings to determine whether Nixon had authorized an effort to spy on the Democratic National Committee's headquarters. What's more, Nixon had secretly recorded incriminating conversations with top staffers.

The whole scandal mattered little to Birdie at this point. His departure date was June 9, and he had already started packing his Bug. On his way out of town, he attended a party at Mick Ryan's houseboat on the Columbia River. An old girlfriend was there, and she provided amphetamine tablets to help him complete the three-hundred-mile trip in one shot.

Birdie took US Highway 26 over Mt. Hood into Central Oregon and then pointed south toward Crater Lake where he could access the park through the fabled "east entrance." When he reached Chemult, north of Klamath Falls, he was bleary eyed and tired, and it was 1:00 a.m. After another hour, he saw a sign that indicated he was approaching Klamath Falls. "Damn," he said aloud, "I missed the turnoff."

What he didn't know was that the east entrance to Crater Lake National Park, constructed by the US Army Corps of Engineers in 1913, had been closed since 1956 because of a decline in visitors entering from that direction. Consequently, he turned westward toward the south entrance into the park. Soon the hallucinations grew increasingly more intense, adding to his distorted state of mind in the pitch-black darkness. With no idea where he was, he entered the park and negotiated the long, windy incline to Crater Lake.

When he finally saw a sign that read Visitor Parking, he pulled over, rolled out his sleeping bag, and fell asleep on the ground next to the Bug. Soon after, the sun rose, but he kept snoozing until he heard the chatter of visitors. Peeking from his bag, he couldn't believe what he had done: in the darkness, he had positioned himself dangerously close to the edge of the rim next to a sharp, fifteen-hundred-foot drop into the lake. "Holy shit," he whispered. "That was close." Recovering from that grim thought, he fully absorbed the moment. The sun shone, the air was fresh, and the view of Crater Lake—the bluest lake he had ever seen—took his breath away.

A couple of tourists volunteered to help him start his VW, and he drove off to Crater Lake Lodge where he was instructed to report for duty.

Seasonal park service and lodge employees comprised a large, temporary community of young people who joined the relatively small group of permanent employees living and working at the park year-round. The boat crew had the good fortune to have their own spacious facility at park headquarters, three miles below the rim, which featured a large dorm space, a Great Room with a fireplace and furniture, and more than twenty individual bedrooms.

When Birdie arrived at his new quarters, P.T. introduced him to the other tour guides, Chaz Reese and Jerry Egovora. Chaz, a tour guide veteran from the previous summer, was a former sailor stationed in Manila during the Vietnam War, and he knew his way around a boat. A native of Gold Beach, Chaz lived in Springfield and attended Lane Community College, training as a respiratory therapist. Jerry, a former sailor and a jack-of-all-trades from Albany, was a dead ringer for Jimmy Buffet.

On their first day, the crew attended a meeting to learn about roles, responsibilities, and their work routines, which involved a daily trip around the rim to the trail at Cleetwood Cove, about eleven miles. They would then hike the 1.1-mile trail down to the boat dock, dropping seven hundred feet in elevation. An easy downhill hike in the morning, it became an exhausting uphill workout at day's end, followed by a twenty-two-mile drive back around the rim, a one-way road, to dinner at the cafeteria at Rim Village.

Rim Village was the focal point where most visitors and tourists stopped before continuing on their journey to their next destination. The rim itself featured historic Crater Lake Lodge, built in 1911, not long after Crater Lake was designated a national park by President Theodore Roosevelt. Rim Village also hosted a visitor's center, a campground, a combination store and gift shop, and a cafeteria for tourists and employees.

The upstairs portion of Rim Village featured the Wineglass Bar and Grill, where patrons could acquire better culinary fare than what was available in the cafeteria. At Crater Lake Lodge, the fourth floor housed most of the seasonal employees who worked for Crater Lake Lodge, Inc. The other floors were the exclusive realm of well-heeled tourists. The lodge's restaurant, the Dining Room, was commonly known as the DR by employees. For seasonal employees, only a serious date would merit a dinner at the upscale DR. The main floor of the lodge accommodated a small bar dubbed the Caldera Room.

On Birdie's first day of work, the crew drove their designated vehicle, a blue Ford 250 pickup with a six-pack cab, to the cafeteria for breakfast, followed by their first trip to Cleetwood Cove. There, they met the lodge boat supervisor, Ron Jackson, a salty old sailor and marina owner from Portland who was close friends with Mr. Fisher, along with Will Jackson, Ron's son, and Joe Kaynak, the boat mechanic. Ron and Joe served in the US Navy together in the South Pacific and witnessed action at the Battle of Midway during World War II. Will wasn't much older than the boat crew, but he was co-owner of his dad's marina in Portland and a skilled sailor.

The first few days, the crew hiked down to the lake, while the supervisors rode a small tractor-trailer packed with an inflatable craft and a small outboard motor. The first order of business was to motor the inflatable to Wizard Island, where they would then launch the tour boats from their berths in dry dock and return to Cleetwood Cove. In total, four forty-eight-foot tour boats were stored on the island in "snow-worthy" boathouses for the winter.

From the rim, the boat houses were visible with the human eye, but you had to know where to look. Birdie learned that distances and dimensions could be oddly deceiving at high altitude. Next, the crew and supervisors prepared to launch the other three tour boats so they could all return to Cleetwood Cove. The four tour boats would remain moored in Cleetwood Cove until the season ended in early September.

At the end of the first day, the crew drove back to Rim Village for dinner and more orientation sessions.

Tours wouldn't begin until the Fourth of July, so the boat crew's routine for the first few days was to prepare the boats, construct the ticket shack, and conduct general maintenance on the boats.

That night, Birdie had a dream about Neil Moriarity. It had been one year since Neil had been killed in that tragic car accident, and Birdie reflected.

Birdie and Neil had attended OLPS since first grade, but they weren't in the same classroom until third grade. They hung together with Lu' and P.T. and played on the same Catholic Youth Organization sports teams. In 1966, Neil and Birdie founded the Passing Clouds, a rock group, as many youngsters of the era had done, inspired by bands like the Beatles, the Rolling Stones, the Who, and others.

The band congregated in the Moriarity family basement, a safe haven for ne'er-do-wells looking for fun and excitement. The room had an unadorned concrete ground floor, and the pool table dominated the space. Other fun features included a card table and an 8-track cassette player powered by a 12-volt battery. The band practiced in that space, occasionally to the chagrin of the rest of the Moriarity family.

Besides Neil on drums and Birdie covering the bass guitar, there were three other lads from the Class of '67 in the band: Mick Ryan on backup vocals and tambourine, and Jim Mitchell and Sean Rowell on lead and rhythm guitars. The band was decent enough to play at the OLPS graduation party for the Class of '67 and other middle schools, but by 1969, the group had disbanded.

Birdie and Neil stuck together throughout high school, and they were particularly adept at mischief. They were often caught in the act but, amazingly, with few repercussions. Both cited the adrenaline rush as the cause of their penchant for shenanigans, evidenced by their boldness to steal the vestibule rugs out of the OLPS church to carpet the back of Neil's '53 Chevy panel van.

As Birdie reflected, he sighed. Much had happened in the past year. He had escaped the long arm of the US military and the war in Vietnam in an elaborate but complicated evasion of the authorities. He had been reprieved by Lady Fortune and now had a fresh start at one of the most beautiful spots on the planet—Crater Lake National Park. He was determined to turn over a new leaf.

Soon the boat crew settled into their daily routine: a three-mile drive from park headquarters to the rim for breakfast and then a drive to the top of Cleetwood Cove. Whoever worked in the ticket shack that day pumped the gas down the hill while the others hiked to the docks to prepare for the onslaught of tourists, known collectively as *touri*.

The first boat left at 9:00 a.m., followed by those at 10:30 a.m., 12:00 noon, 1:30 p.m., and 3:00 p.m. A "Wizard Island Express" was the last boat of the day to pick up stragglers left on the island. At 5:00 p.m., the crew hiked back up the trail for the drive back to their quarters before embarking for dinner.

At first, the crew ate exclusively at the cafeteria, but after receiving their first paychecks, they could splurge at the Wineglass upstairs on pizza and pitchers of sangria. The crew would work seven days a week "because of the short season," as Mr. Fisher had noted in his letter. Consequently, every day was Friday, so they partied accordingly.

On the morning of the Fourth of July, the fair weather changed, and it inexplicably snowed. Usually one of the two biggest days of the summer for tours at Crater Lake National Park, the crew's workday was scuttled by about six inches of snow blanketing Rim Village. Arriving at the rim for breakfast, the crew was told to return to their quarters for the day.

"We get the day off!" said P.T. "Let's go to Klamath Falls!"

Everybody agreed, and dumping their work vehicle at their quarters, they jumped into P.T.'s car and hit the road south. The first settlement down the hill from the lake was Fort Klamath, home of an old fort used by the US Cavalry to patrol the Klamath Basin, which served as the reservation for Modoc and Klamath natives. The Modocs, led by Captain Jack, were combatants in one of the last of the so-called "Indian Wars" in the West.

Fascinated by the story behind the Modocs and their battle with the US Cavalry, Birdie had read *Wigwam and Warpath* by Alfred B. Meacham in a Pacific Northwest history class at Mt. Hood Community College. The Modoc tribe was a branch of the larger group of Klamath natives in Southern Oregon and Northern California in the days before white explorers and settlers. Captain Jack and the Modocs were a peaceful group, but they often had to contend with the shortcomings of white Indian agents and the overbearing dominance of the Klamath tribe. The agents, however, considered the Modocs a perpetual annoyance and had them resettled on a reservation.

The Modocs lasted about a year on the reservation, but they pined for their ancestral home near Lost River, so they abandoned the reservation and returned home. Finally, a new superintendent ordered the Modocs back to the reservation, encouraged by a force of about forty soldiers, who confronted Jack and the Modocs. The commander instructed the Modocs to throw down their guns. Every Modoc complied but one, a fellow named "Scarface Charlie," who maintained his pistol in his holster. When one soldier attempted to physically disarm the Modoc while shouting obscenities, Charlie fired two shots. The cavalry responded with gunfire, and the Modocs retaliated with rifle fire.

The Modocs escaped with their families to the Lava Beds near Tulelake, California, an extensive volcanic feature that provided extremely defensible positions in battle. The tribe took advantage of the unique formations, using numerous caves and tunnels dotting the rugged landscape. They fought the soldiers to an impasse for five months against ten times as many combatants. After a particularly fierce battle, the government sent a commission under General Edward Canby, a Civil War hero, to negotiate peace with the Modocs.

The tribe agreed, but they were willing to meet with only two of their representatives: Frank Riddle and his Modoc wife, Winema, who would coordinate the peace talks. The Modocs insisted on negotiating with Canby and his entourage and scheduled to meet near Canby's council tent unarmed. Before the meeting, the Modocs voted to kill the white leaders against Jack's advice, insisting that they would then leave for good. Jack scoffed at the suggestion, noting that others would replace them and in greater numbers.

Despite dire warnings from Winema, Canby and his

companions departed for the Modoc camp. Arriving with his party, Canby sensed a tense atmosphere, and Jack seemed ill at ease. One soldier noticed the absence of Modoc women and suggested a trap. The pressure increased until Jack gave the fatal signal. He shot General Canby, and several of the soldiers were killed, though several escaped. The outrage caused by these assassinations would prove Captain Jack's predictions to be true. The Modocs escaped back to the Lava Beds, but the cavalry eventually succeeded in cutting off their water supply.

The Modocs fled to the south but were apprehended and tried by a military commission at Fort Klamath. The prosecution was convincing, and the defense was pathetic. Captain Jack's defense summation offered a rational plea to simply remain on their land in peace. Unfortunately, the end for Captain Jack and the others came on the gallows at Fort Klamath. For Birdie, it was another example of paradox in life. Both Canby and Captain Jack wanted peace, yet their lives ended in violent death (Meacham, Alfred B. *Wigwam and Warpath: or the Royal Chief in Chains*. Boston: J. P. Dale, 1875).

As the boat crew left Fort Klamath, they passed a small, unremarkable restaurant called Gramma Jones Fried Chicken that sat next to the Wood River. The establishment would become a favorite spot to take the girls for dinner. Down on the Klamath flatlands and marshes, Klamath Lake, the largest lake in Oregon, appeared on the right before entering Klamath Falls. Once there, the crew hit a few stores for groceries and supplies. K-Falls had a G.I. Joe's, so everybody stocked up on fishing gear, cook stoves, knives, coolers, and other essentials for camping, hiking, and climbing.

Mission completed, the crew stopped at the Red Garter Saloon in northern K-Falls on the way out of town. The sign advertising pizza presented an immediate call to action. The establishment was spacious, but the clientele appeared rough and rowdy. Half the place was filled with rednecks, and the other half was comprised of Modoc and Klamath natives. The boat crew ordered pizza and a couple of pitchers, and Chaz and P.T. dared to challenge a couple of the natives in a game of pool.

The natives were good natured, but the rednecks unleased a crude barrage of insults at both the natives and the boat crew, but nobody took the bait. Instead, they all had a delightful discussion about Crater Lake. One mentioned that most Klamath and Modoc natives, even those who worked at the park, found Crater Lake "eerie." "A vague uneasiness can be haunting," he said, "especially in bad weather. Wind howls, and clouds sweep in quickly, and you suddenly can't tell what's down in that hole. You want to get away fast."

"What about the stories of a giant crawfish in the lake?" Birdie asked.

"Well, that's nonsense, of course," the Modoc lad replied, "but that is the legend. The lake does appear to do funny things to people. Some tourists walk over the rim and disappear. Spooky. We tend to stay away from the lake itself."

Once the boat crew had a full helping of pizza and tired of the good ole boys, they returned to their bunkhouse at park headquarters.

The Klamath lad's stories of "bad juju" about Crater Lake were gleaned from many variations of native legends. The indigenous inhabitants of the lowlands south and east of the mountain called it Llao's Mountain. Crater Lake was a powerful, mystical place and the home of Llao, who resided inside the mountain. Llao, the supreme ruler of the underworld was assisted by his minions, a collection of lesser spirits who could change their worldly forms at will. The native tribes settled in the basins nearby Mt. Mazama as the Pleistocene melt filled the giant lakes and marshes. Humans were understandably fearful of the mountain, then one of the great stratovolcanoes of the world. They revered the peak, and tribal shamans wove tales of mystery about the dwelling of Llao.

While Llao occupied the grim mass north of the marshes, Skell—the benign god of the earth and the sky—ruled to the south on the lofty, white dome known today as Mt. Shasta. Skell had won the heart of a Klamath princess with his goodness and light, according to legend. Rejected and humiliated by the daughter of a Klamath chieftain, the lovelorn Llao sought revenge, trying to destroy her people with a curse of fire. He battled with Skell, her protector, who ultimately vanquished the prince of darkness once and for all.

Crater Lake was no overnight sensation, according to Howel Williams. Over the course of time, a small lake eventually appeared in the caldera: first as a series of small pools, then larger pools with connecting channels, and finally as a singular, continuous and ever-deepening body of water. Once Mt. Mazama collapsed within itself in a terminal cataclysm, the resulting caldera resembled a visage of hell from Dante's "Inferno"—a seething bottom of molten debris, fragments of sharp rock, and pools of bubbling mud. Episodes of glacial accumulation alternated with periods of volcanic eruption. Lava flows and showers dissipated the glaciers on the slopes of the caldera, creating torrents of melted water flowing into the newly formed basin. Williams wrote:

> "As passing clouds unburdened themselves of their moisture, the level of the lake gradually rose. Four-fifths of the water fell directly into the lake as rain or snow; the rest was supplied by small torrents cascading into the basin from the encircling cliffs" (Williams, Howel. Crater Lake: *The Story of Its Origin*. Berkeley: University of California Press, 1970).

Williams estimated that it took perhaps thousands of years for rainwater and snow to fill Crater Lake to its present level. The elevation of the lake averages about 6,150 feet above sea level and is nearly two thousand feet deep at its deepest point. Since there are no inlets or outlets to the lake, its level varies little. The lake level remains balanced by a constant cycle of precipitation and evaporation. The depth is such that Crater Lake has frozen solid on the surface only twice in recorded history.

As the deepest body of fresh water in the United States, the immense depth of the lake acts as a thermal reservoir that absorbs and traps the heat, maintaining the water temperature at 55 degrees Fahrenheit on its surface and 38 degrees at its bottom during the summer. All told, it took thousands of years for the caldera to transform into the heavenly views of the stunningly beautiful indigo pool that exists today. Williams' book also covered the points of interest on the inside of the caldera wall.

The tour circuit started at Cleetwood Cove and proceeded counterclockwise around the lake. The first point of interest was Steel Bay, named after the park's champion and first superintendent, William Gladstone Steel, followed by Llao Rock, a giant dacite lava flow that filled a mountain valley on the west side of the lake. The feature resembled a giant black bird from across the lake. Next up along the tour was the Devil's Backbone, an old dike or lava feeder that helped to grow the mountain.

Just past the Devil's Backbone was Skell Channel, a narrow waterway separating the caldera wall from Wizard Island. Circling around the island past Fumarole Bay, the boats arrived at the awaiting docks adjacent to the boathouses in Governor's Bay on Wizard Island. After dropping off and/or picking up tourists, the ride continued to the Sinnott Overlook at Rim Village, where tourists above could view the lake.

Next, Chaski Slide, a giant landslide that sluffed down the incline from the top of the rim about halfway to the lake, featured waterfalls from snowmelt inside the caldera wall. Continuing counterclockwise, the next point of interest was the Phantom Ship, an eerie rock formation resembling a pirate ship that was actually an old feeder dike. As the tour continued, the boats cruised under Sun Notch and Kerr Notch, two river valleys comprising low points along the rim. The Pumice Castle, a unique formation resembling an orange palace, hovered a few hundred feet over the Grotto Cove, a small inlet with a rock formation that appeared similar to a Madonna and child.

The last leg of the tour followed a beeline back to Cleetwood Cove, passing the Wineglass, a rockslide, and the Palisades, a giant billowing lava flow, the lowest point on the rim at 507 feet above the lake. As the returning boat approached the dock, the next boat simultaneously disembarked at Cleetwood Cove for another tour.

Despite all the interesting features on the caldera wall, tourists most commonly asked two questions: "Are there fish in the lake?" and "Why is the lake so blue?" Initially, the National Park Service introduced many varieties of fish in the early part of the twentieth century, including freshwater shrimp. However, only two species survived: kokanee salmon and trout. The dearth of other fish could be attributed to the fact that little food existed. What little feed was available near the shoreline was consumed by the smaller kokanee salmon. The trout subsequently fed off the salmon, which existed in greater numbers. The deep-blue hue resulted from the sheer depth of Crater Lake. When light struck the surface on a sunny day, all the colors of the rainbow were reflected back toward the sky. The blue wavelength, however, was absorbed by the water, hence the deep indigo effect.

On occasion, boat crew members stayed late to fish for those elusive German brown trout. The crew became well versed in conducting tours armed with such information, but at the end of the day, it was all about parties. With so many college students working for the season in the vicinity, a party could be found almost every night. The male-female quotient of those working at the park that summer favored the boat crew.

At one party, Birdie became enamored with a girl from Western Washington University, an attractive coed in the mold of Audrey Hepburn. He even let her drive his boat briefly on a tour to win her favor, but she turned out to be a straight edge, so he lost interest. The poor girl, who was mildly offended by the slight, rebounded with someone else. At another party, Birdie started making waves at a drunken soiree at Cabin 52 with Jan Bradley, a childhood friend from OLPS. They retreated to her room on the fourth floor of Crater Lake Lodge that she shared with three other girls. Much to their surprise, they found three guys sharing beds with the other three gals.

It was a strange night of laughter and sexual escapades. Jan always had been reticent to "do it" with Birdie, but this night, she acquiesced willingly, even eagerly. Inevitably, Birdie had to pee, so he dared venture into the hallway, looking for the restroom. Mrs. Fisher was patrolling the fourth floor, making sure all her "girls" were safe, and that night, she was on the prowl. The boat crew had already established a reputation as lecherous drunks and ne'er-do-wells. Birdie used extreme caution to avoid being seen. He made it back to the room without incident.

A few days later, Birdie met Julie Jane Stone, a cute, blond coed from the University of Colorado who worked as a maid at the cabins. JJ, as she was known, was only seventeen, but she had started college early after skipping a couple of grades in elementary school. With an advanced aptitude for academics, she planned to be a lawyer like her father. For both Birdie and JJ, it was love at first sight. They went everywhere together after hours.

The Fishers, always the gracious hosts, did their best to offer wholesome distractions for lodge guests, like skits and musical acts, and dances for employees from time to time. At lodge-sponsored dances in the school gym at Steel Circle, Birdie and JJ often made the scene. Afterward, they would adjourn to the boat crew quarters and commandeer one of the private rooms. On her days off, JJ came down to the lake for Birdie's tours. She too enjoyed fishing, so after work, the lovebirds piloted the boat to Grotto Cove to seek the elusive German brown trout.

In addition to lodge parties and dances, the "parkies" (seasonal park service employees) had socials, much more unregulated than lodge events. Their cabins were mere steps from the boat crew quarters. The most infamous, Cabin 52, sponsored at least one gig a week. The hosts mixed a big bowl of grape juice with generous amounts of vodka and Everclear. Other parties were conducted at park service quarters at the north entrance to Crater Lake National Park. However, those events could be problematic for lodge employees who had to circumnavigate the rim drive to return to the lodge late at night, an additional thirty-five miles. As a result, few braved the journey except for the boat crew and a few others.

Birdie's mom was experiencing a particularly rough patch during the summer of 1973. Dad had left home, this time for good, and he filed for a divorce after twenty-three years together. Before Birdie left Portland for Crater Lake, his dad invited him to Sneaky Pete's, a dive bar on NE Sixtieth and Glisan to break the news of the divorce.

Birdie wasn't surprised. His response was planned long in advance. "The divorce will be for the best," he said matter-of-factly. "You're not good for her health."

Never a particularly articulate fellow, his dad was rendered mute at Birdie's comment, but his uncomfortable mission had been accomplished. After a couple of beers, they parted ways amicably. Now that Birdie had left the house, and with Emile already on his own, his mom was living in the family home with the siblings remaining: Douglas, Carlotta, and Stevie.

Despite her sadness because of the divorce, Birdie's mom

gained the freedom to travel, spend money on herself and others, and generally enjoy her new life. She now could do whatever she pleased, and she planned a trip to Crater Lake. Birdie called his mom one day and mentioned that he and JJ were taking a trip to the beach soon. His long-term plans were to move to Boulder with JJ and apply for admission to the journalism program at the University of Colorado.

She responded with a letter on July 22.

Dear Birdie,
Shortly after your call on Thursday, the operator called me back. She said that she couldn't reach you, and there was twelve minutes overtime and a charge of $2.70 plus $.27 tax. She asked for your name and the additional charge is on our bill (naturally, your father said that I must pay it!). When I come visit in August, I hope you have the time so that I can see Klamath Falls too. I dread the thought of you going to the beach. I have recollections of the worry, time, and expense of the Tillamook episode!

Dad found and mailed your license tags on Friday morning. Naturally, he had me pay for the postage! Gramma was delighted to receive your call! She called me immediately. When you send me some of the money you owe me, please get a money order. Please get it here soon. Uncle Bruce McInnes mentioned that your Aunt Mace McInnes is not coming to Portland. I understand it's because of the gas shortage. Make certain you have enough gas when you go to Bandon and Boulder.

I'm still following Watergate in *The Oregonian*, *Newsweek*, and *Time*. The press is raking Nixon over the coals. Stevie, Carlotta, and I are going to see Disney on Parade at the Memorial Coliseum today. This comes once a year, and the girls have been waiting to see it. Take care.

Love,
Mom

Even though Birdie was aware of the implications of "Julie's" letter exposing his dad's youthful indiscretion, the picture had finally become clear with the impending divorce. Told he was premature at birth, the math had never made sense to him. His parents were married on May 23, 1952, and he was born six months later. Weighing less than five pounds, he was barely big enough to avoid an incubator.

Julie's letter had provided a key piece to the puzzle. For example, the missive explained why his dad's family was absent on his own wedding day. His mom's parents displayed obvious disgust in the wedding pictures taken that day. If looks could kill, his dad would have been dead right where he stood. Birdie imagined this scenario: after his dad impregnated a teenage girl in North Portland while he attended college, most of his family disowned or avoided him.

The poor girl's parents relegated her to a home for unwed mothers where she gave birth and then placed the child up for adoption. She later married and had a family of her own. Subsequently, when Birdie's mom became pregnant, his dad likely tried to avoid marriage, but his mom's parents were upset. Italian immigrants, they considered this sort of disgrace unacceptable, so they acted upon the news.

When his mom's pregnancy became obvious because of morning sickness, Birdie's gramma noticed right away and confronted her. Mom obediently identified the guilty suspect when quizzed. Once Grandpa Carl became involved, he and Gramma contacted the other grandparents of the baby who would become Birdie. Their conversation likely went something like this: "Your son has impregnated our daughter, and under Italian tradition, that means he must marry her immediately." His dad's parents agreed and forced his hand. Even though his dad wasn't interested in marrying Birdie's mom, he agreed, and the date was set.

The union would produce five children and a lifetime of work and misery for his mom and consequently all the kids. When the siblings were old enough, they all moved out. The verbal and physical abuse that had raged for years had become unbearable. Paradoxically, Birdie's mom, who at age twenty-three had wanted a husband so badly that she married his dad, was finally liberated. It opened a whole new world for her.

In late July, the lake was choppy during a three-day rainstorm, so the boat crew conducted primary maintenance on the main boathouse on Wizard Island, which had replaced the one that burned to the ground during the summer of 1972. The new structure had been hastily rebuilt, so as the season waned, there was still much painting and other improvements needed. The fire had left debris, particularly metal roofing and rusted engine blocks from old tour boats replaced with newer models.

Occasionally, Birdie took his breaks on the dock rereading *Catcher in the Rye* and *On the Road* by Jack Kerouac. Much like Kerouac, Birdie envisioned a life on the highways and byways of America when he could find time and a decent automobile. He anticipated his trips with JJ to the beach and later to Colorado.

By August, the annual Moonlight Boat Cruise, an event inexplicably sanctioned by Mr. Fisher, was offered as a treat for employees. The crew would spend a long day on the lake, yet one and all anticipated the after-hours event with great enthusiasm. Enough participants registered to fill three boats, so Birdie, P.T., and Chaz boarded eager lodge employees at dark and departed Cleetwood Cove.

After docking on Wizard Island, some employees climbed to the cinder cone on top under a moon that illuminated the entire caldera. Birdie and JJ retreated to a private spot near the top and gazed at the full moon in wonderment as they pondered their future together. Meanwhile, others frolicked around the island under the brightly illuminated caldera. On the way back to Cleetwood Cove, the boats inched toward the edge of Chaski Slide, providing an unexpected shower from creeks running off the snowfields above. Incredibly, the event went off without a hitch, and everybody had fun.

When their road trip arrived, JJ and Birdie packed the Bug and departed for the Oregon Coast. JJ had been anxious to see the ocean for as long as she could remember. Birdie practically grew up on the Oregon Coast in Lincoln City, but he hadn't explored the Southern Oregon coast. Leaving via the north entrance, they followed the headwaters of the Umpqua River to US Interstate 5 and turned onto an obscure state road toward Bandon, Oregon.

In Bandon, they walked barefoot on the beach among the large rocks in the surf and discussed their future together. The lovebirds rented a room at the Bandon Beach Motel and enjoyed a full day of exploring the town and visiting the shops. After they ate dinner at a seafood restaurant, they spent the rest of the night wrestling with one another in amorous love. The next day, they drove south on the coast through Gold Beach and Brookings, dipping into Northern California to Highway 199, which angled north back into Oregon. From Grants Pass, they pointed easterly through Gold Hill and Prospect to the south entrance of Crater Lake National Park, arriving late in the day.

Meanwhile, in political news of the day, the Watergate scandal continued to unravel when former White House aid Alexander Butterfield informed the US Senate Watergate Committee that President Nixon had secretly recorded recriminating conversations. The administration continued to disintegrate as summer waned, leading to other disastrous news for the president. This ominous sign for the country would presage troubling times for Birdie as well.

One day, the boat crew learned about an upcoming total lunar eclipse, and a plan was hatched: the entire crew would join their girlfriends and view the eclipse on one of the boats. Keeping the boats moored at Cleetwood Cove, they played hearts and pinochle and waited. Then they waited some more, followed by more waiting. Nothing happened. "Did we miss it?" Jerry asked no one in particular. They threw in the towel at about 4:00 a.m. and went to sleep. The next morning, Birdie and JJ slept late only to be rudely awakened by Bill Jackson and Joe Kaynak on a surprise visit. Birdie figured he was in trouble, but the incident faded without fanfare. Other troubling times were ahead, though, and Birdie's life would continue to spiral downward.

Birdie's buddy from Portland, Chuck Schneider, had driven to Crater Lake for a visit. In a moment of poor judgment, Birdie allowed him to drive the boat in Skell Channel, where the water was exceedingly shallow. Just before Birdie resumed the wheel, everyone onboard heard a loud thump followed by other unsettling mechanical sounds. Birdie grabbed the wheel from Chuck and struggled to turn starboard so he could veer left and land on Wizard Island at the appointed time. Something was seriously wrong with the boat. He calmly announced, "To the left, we have Wizard Island rising 763 feet above the lake. The island has a trail that you can climb to the top if you're interested. A later boat can take you back to Cleetwood Cove." Fortunately, another tour boat was moored at the dock, so Birdie had his passengers disembark from his boat to continue the tour.

This time, he knew he was in big trouble. The propeller and the keel of the boat had been damaged by the rock hidden below the surface in Skell Channel, disabling the craft until parts could arrive from Portland. On the trail up to the rim, Birdie had that shitty feeling he had when subjected to a tribunal with his dad. This time it was Mr. Fisher who summoned him as soon as he learned what had happened. His "office" that day was the bar in the Caldera Room, and he had been drinking.

"I understand the boat is damaged," he said. "It's going to cost a lot of money."

"I'm sorry," Birdie said. "I edged a little too close to the shoreline in Skell Channel."

"That's no excuse," Fisher said. "You know how to drive the boat."

Birdie held his tongue and hoped for the best.

"You can go now," Fisher said, disgusted.

Luckily for Birdie, Fisher let the issue die, but he deducted Birdie's deposit and cancelled his bonus at the end of the season.

Birdie's next misfortune was a sprained ankle when he

jumped from the gas pump on the bank onto the boat dock. The sprain was so severe that he was unable to hike up the trail. P.T. coaxed the tractor into gear and carted Birdie up to the trailhead, where he met a ranger who drove him to the lodge for transport to Klamath Falls. The lodge limo driver, a friend of Birdie's, rushed him to the emergency room at the hospital adjacent to Oregon Technical Institute. As he anguished, the X-rays showed the bone wasn't broken, but it was severely sprained and would require a cast. He would be obliged to ride the tractor, but even that task had its own hazards. A week later, the tractor lost its brakes and barreled down the hillside. P.T. yelled, "Jump!" and both leapt from the tractor, which came to an abrupt stop near the bottom. Shaken but relieved, the crew yarded the tractor back on the trail with a hand winch so that repairs could be made.

Birdie's next disaster occurred when returning from a party at the north entrance to Crater Lake National Park. Rather than take the long route, he turned off his headlights under the full moon and knowingly violated the law by driving the wrong way on the one-way road. His error in judgment proved to be a costly mistake. When he arrived at the resumption of the two-way road, a well-concealed park ranger flipped on his lights and flashers.

Caught red-handed and red-faced, Birdie received a reckless driving ticket. He would need to appear before a judge in Medford two weeks hence. The fine was listed as $300, which Birdie could hardly afford. On the bright side, he was relieved that the ranger didn't conduct a sobriety test when he received his ticket. Toward the end of August, Birdie began to suffer from depression and was drinking more heavily, showing up at lodge parties and carousing with other women, which JJ noticed. Naturally, she wasn't pleased, and she decided to take a hiatus from him.

Birdie noticed that she had noticed and was immediately remorseful. He apologized and tried to make amends. JJ relented, and they went out to dinner several times as the summer season waned. He seemed to be on the rebound and felt better when they kissed at the end of the night, yet he had a nagging sense that the damage had been done. *What a fucking idiot!* he thought. *The girl of my dreams, and I piss the whole relationship away carelessly.*

The weather deteriorated more consistently prior to Labor Day, and the boat crew spent their remaining days on the island conducting maintenance and tidying up the boathouse in preparation for dry docking the tour boats before winter. The rush to finish the new boathouse before the snows flew the previous summer had left a mess.

The previous season, when they were cleaning up the old boathouse site, Chaz and P.T. had piled the aluminum roofing and other debris on a launch dock. They had towed the dock around Wizard Island with a tour boat and dumped the charred metal into the lake under orders from management. P.T. recalled, "The dock was about fifty feet long and eight feet wide, and we stacked the junk to about shoulder height. We took the dock just far enough around the island so that we couldn't be observed from the Rim Village area. We dumped two loads of junk and were specifically told to not mention a word of it to anyone."

This season would be no different. Once again, the boat crew received orders to clean up the island around the boathouse and dump three old engine blocks. Birdie and P.T. were tasked to tow a rowboat with an engine block with another rowboat equipped with an outboard motor to a point about two miles from the docks. The idea was to send it to the depths of Crater Lake.

About a mile off Wizard Island, the boat with the engine block began gulping water over its stern. Birdie pulled out his knife to cut the rope but too late. Thrown airborne as the lake swallowed their rowboat, both hit the water with a splash. Startled and gasping for air, they frantically splashed about but regained their composure and swam toward the island. An unlikely task: both knew that hypothermia would soon overcome them. Spotting them from the island, Chaz hastily fired up a tour boat and drove full throttle, finding them in the water and pulling them out.

"You just saved our lives, Chaz," P.T. said, teeth chattering.

He had indeed. The Curse of Llao had struck again. On this occasion, however, the dark forces of Crater Lake had failed to claim its victims.

A few days later, when Birdie's reckless driving court date commenced in Medford, the crew accompanied him to show the poor lad support and attend an outdoor concert. Luckily, Birdie escaped with a reduced charge of careless driving. Afterward, Elvin Bishop, an original member of the Paul Butterfield Blues Band, performed at the Jackson County Fairgrounds. The crew caught his concert and celebrated Birdie's fortunate outcome before returning to Crater Lake.

Birdie's turn of fortune was brief. What happened next was utterly catastrophic. While the boat crew celebrated the end of the season at the Wineglass, JJ and her friend, Jennifer, attended a party at the north entrance cabins. On their way back, they circled around the rim on the dark, moonless night. Rounding a curve near the Mt. Scott trailhead, their car collided with a herd of Roosevelt elk, killing JJ and Jennifer instantly. No one learned about the tragedy until the next morning when Rim Village awoke shocked and disillusioned. Rim Village buzzed with authorities of all stripes, most notably the Federal Bureau of Investigation.

The park shut down for a day, and the lodge employees, park staff, and boat crew were interviewed. The news affected Birdie in ways he never could have imagined; inconsolable and guilt-ridden, he was unable to sleep and suffered panic attacks, wondering what he could have done to prevent such a disaster. He spent the next twenty-four hours in a fog. Like a cold wind on the lake, the news swept through the community, transforming the Crater Lake community into a zombie nation.

The Fishers flew grief counselors from Portland to Medford, and the lodge limo driver transported them to the lake to meet with employees while authorities continued to investigate, but the verdict was clear; it was simply an unfortunate accident. At the end of the week, lodge employees packed their belongings to leave for their next destination. Most went back to college, but others had jobs lined up or other endeavors. Birdie and the rest of the boat crew loaded their stuff and prepared for departure.

On his way out, Birdie stopped at the lodge to say goodbye to those who remained. When she saw him walk into the lodge, Jerry's girlfriend, Linda, stopped Birdie. "I have something for you, but I wasn't sure if I should give it to you."

"Why?" he asked.

"I wasn't sure how it would affect you," she replied, "but I think you should have it, so here it is."

The note read, "Dear Birdie, we played our summer without rules and won. Love, JJ."

Tears welled in Birdie's eyes, and he gave Linda a long hug. "Thank you, Linda. I really appreciate it."

CHAPTER EIGHT

Welcome to Eugene

Fall 1973: Before Birdie departed from Crater Lake for Portland, he felt compelled to visit the accident site near Redcloud Cliff on the northeast side of the lake. Late departing from the bunkhouse, he arrived at the scene near the Mt. Scott trailhead at sunset. He could see skid marks from the tires and little else. With darkness approaching, he knew he wouldn't make it far that day on his journey back to the City of Roses.

Leaving the park through the north entrance, Birdie camped at nearby Diamond Lake, a national forest campground with tent sites and showers. He pitched his tent in a designated campsite and tried to sleep, but his mind was awash with images of JJ. After a restless—and mostly sleepless—night, he arose at dawn for a quick shower and plucked a towel from his backpack. Adjusting the flow on the showerhead, he heard JJ's voice as clear as if she was in the shower with him: "I'm sorry, Birdie. Don't worry. I love you. Please forgive me." Birdie began sobbing with grief.

Dumbfounded at hearing her voice aloud, Birdie's knees buckled, yet he somehow maintained his balance. He could hardly believe what he had heard, yet he knew he heard both her voice and, more importantly, her message. He wept for five minutes until he collected himself. He cried aloud, "Of course I forgive you, JJ! I love you!"

With his gear packed into the VW, Birdie once again hit the road bound for Portland. Renewed by his ethereal experience in the shower, he pondered returning home. He knew it would be hard to adjust after several months at Crater Lake. He was not the same individual who left Portland. His family and friends hadn't witnessed his experiences, and none were there when he lost JJ. He had changed. It would be impossible to explain the events that had changed him, yet he pressed on to Portland. Where else would he go? He missed his family, but his future was now unclear, except for one certainty. He knew he must return to school.

As he drove, he remembered something he had once heard before: "Nobody escapes the wonderful or horrible things in life. That is the space between life and death."

"Back to school." The expression conjured up memories of that long-dreaded yet long-awaited day for OLPS students to return to the classroom at summer's end. Three months could seem like three years to a youngling. Unlike public school kids who received new clothes for a new school year, those in Catholic schools could look forward to another year of the same wardrobe: blue shirts and salt 'n' pepper cords for boys, and blue plaid jumpers with a white blouse for girls. Younger siblings from a large family, as many were, would inherit their new school duds from an older sibling. Pretty exciting. On the upside, returning to school could be invigorating, a chance to reconnect with old mates and meet new ones added to the class rosters. The new year would also introduce a new teacher, be it lay instructor or nun. You never knew what you might get: an old lay teacher, a young nun, an old nun, or a young lay teacher. It was one big crap shoot.

Most in Birdie's class attended OLPS for eight years, the longest commitment of their young lives at that point. Many, however, would exit Catholic schools after their experience at OLPS for a public high school. Some would attend one of the half dozen Catholic high schools in the area, all segregated by sex. Females attended St. Mary's Academy, Holy Child, Marycrest, or St. Mary of the Valley. Males attended Central Catholic, Jesuit, or North Catholic. That prospect would not be an option for many who had attended OLPS for so long, especially those who had suffered through the onerous philosophy of maximum restraint and minimum responsibility. Many transferred to a public high school where, ironically, they would encounter the exact opposite philosophy: minimum restraint and maximum responsibility.

Birdie, on the other hand, had won a scholarship to Jesuit, a prestigious Catholic high school, by taking first place in the school's speech contest. The Jesuit Speech Contest, held annually for the dozens of Catholic elementary schools in the Portland-Vancouver metropolitan area, was open to middle schools that fielded a competitive speech team. The contest allowed seventh and eighth graders to compete in three categories of public speaking: extemporaneous, impromptu, and memorized script. For the memorized speech, the categories were serious and humorous.

Impromptu speaking involved delivering a message on the spur of the moment. Contestants were spontaneously asked to speak on a particular subject. Extemporaneous speaking consisted of delivering a speech in a conversational fashion using prepared notes from a selected reading.

Memorized speaking involved the recitation of a written message that the speaker had committed to memory in advance, allowing for eye contact and body language in their delivery. The memorized speech took the most time to prepare, and contestants practiced for weeks, even months, ahead of the event.

Birdie had been recruited by the nuns of OLPS for the speech team based on his speaking abilities in the classroom. One nun in particular, Sister Marie, mentored and coached him. As a seventh grader, he chose the final defense summation of Atticus Finch, who defends an African-American man falsely accused of raping a white woman in *To Kill A Mockingbird* by Harper Lee, for his memorized speech in the serious category. He performed well and placed first among all the seventh graders.

In eighth grade, Birdie tried his hand at comedy and chose "Tonsils" by Bill Cosby. He had to transcribe the bit into written text and practiced the speech for weeks. At the event, he felt confident that he would prevail as the winner once again. When the judges rendered their decisions, three out of four scored him in first place, but one didn't score him at all. He was puzzled by that outcome and asked Sister Marie about the discrepancy. "The judge in question had voiced a bias against African American comedians like Bill Cosby," she sighed. Birdie still placed first at the Jesuit Speech Contest and won the scholarship.

As a result, his parents insisted that he attend Jesuit, a college prep institution, in his own best interests. Eventually, like many others who attended Catholic high school after eight years of parochial elementary education, Birdie abandoned Jesuit after his sophomore year and finished his junior and senior years at Lincoln High, a public school.

When some of his classmates at Jesuit asked why he was transferring, he replied, "Girls." It was the easiest answer.

At OLPS, it was hard to avoid reminders of your own mortality. Sometimes the reminders were graphic, even chilling: the "scourge at the pillar," "the agony in the garden," and "the slaying of Goliath." Don't forget the "crown of thorns." As altar boys, they were reminded about St. Tarcisius, a young martyr who was beaten to death by thugs as he carried the Holy Eucharist to the dying. Horrifying stuff surrounded the classrooms and the church in art and sculpture. Then there were the classroom smells: chalk and chalkboards, pencil lead, markers, and erasers, not to mention the unmistakable aromas coming from the cafeteria—some pleasing, some not.

In addition to attending daily Mass, sometimes twice daily if you were an altar boy, students spent an hour in "religion" class, which usually meant focusing on readings from the Old or New Testament. The environment provided constant reminders of how Catholics celebrated death and bloodshed with eternal salvation as the goal. The graphic depictions of Roman and Jewish brutality were enough to make you wonder why Jesus didn't hate those sons of bitches too.

A favorite of those with an odd sense of humor (practically everybody at Catholic schools) was the "Holy Foreskin," which was passed around Europe until the eighteenth century. The odd relic was believed to be the foreskin of a circumcised Jesus Christ himself. Despite the constant grim reminders of mortality and death, most students became oblivious, and the novelty of a new school year at OLPS faded quickly into the long grind toward Christmas, spring, and finally summer again.

As Birdie drove north toward Portland, he focused on the positive aspects of his summer, appreciating all the good times in light of the horror and trauma of losing JJ. His post-Crater Lake plans had been altered entirely. Instead of driving to Colorado, he found himself on the road back to Portland, a depressing thought. "What am I going to do?" he kept asking himself.

Along the way, he stopped in Eugene to visit high school buddies attending the University of Oregon. He left invigorated from his stay in Eugene. *I could live here*, he thought. He had applied for acceptance to the journalism school at UO but hadn't heard back. Despite its distance from the media centers of America, UO featured one of the top-rated schools of journalism, advertising, and public relations in the country. The school had produced many world-renowned journalists, researchers, and politicians, even Oregon's current governor, Tom McCall, a former newscaster. Plus, Birdie could take advantage of in-state tuition rates instead of paying costly out-of-state fees.

He had an epiphany: he would finish fall quarter at Mt. Hood Community College, which ran through December, and move to Eugene whether he had been accepted or not.

When he arrived in Portland the next day, his family was relieved to see him after his first summer away. Birdie had a stack of mail waiting that he would need to sort. The first one he saw was from Mt. Hood Community College.

It read:

Dear returning student:

With summer rapidly passing and fall approaching, we hope you still plan to attend Mt. Hood Community College. Your appointment date, time, and location are on the enclosed form which you earlier filled out. If you are unable to keep your appointment, you should plan on registering on either September 20 or 21. We look forward to seeing you this coming year.

Birdie had missed his appointment, so he would need to register in another week. Another letter was addressed from UO. It read:

Dear Mr. McInnes:

The enclosed Statement of Admission reflects that you have been accepted for enrollment at the University of Oregon starting in January. You can be sure this notification is sent with genuine pleasure on our part. Now, we hope you honor us by actually becoming a member of the UO student body.

Please find the enclosed instructions relevant to establishing a record of immunization and physical examination at the University Health Center. Do not overlook the presence of your student identification card. In the interim, I hope you are now in possession of sufficient information to direct your decisions and actions. If we may be of further assistance, please feel free to contact us.

Sincerely,
UO Department of Admissions

Birdie was encouraged. With a spot available for fall term at Mt. Hood Community College, he had been accepted at UO to pursue a degree in journalism. His spirits had been lifted by Divine Providence.

Conversely, the Nixon administration continued to crumble under its own hubris. The vice president, Spiro T. Agnew, resigned after pleading no contest to charges of income tax evasion while governor of Maryland. He was fined $10,000 and placed on probation for three years. A few days later, Nixon unleashed the "Saturday Night Massacre." The action raised an outcry for his impeachment.

Meanwhile, Birdie and Lu' continued their studies at Mt. Hood Community College. Birdie signed up for one journalism class, Mass Communication, along with a history class, first-year German, and physical education classes in bowling and badminton.

Birdie learned to bowl in the late sixties when the boys loitered at Mayfair Bowl, a bowling center near SE Eighty-Second and Division Street. Because they looked old enough, they were allowed to enter the facility as long as they had money to play the pinball machines. Occasionally, they even bowled when they could afford it. Smoking was pervasive at Mayfair Bowl, and the lads could get away with it. Smoke hung like a cloud in the air. Even those who didn't smoke left smelling like an ashtray.

Lu' and Birdie hoped to improve their games while taking the bowling class, with sessions held at nearby Gresham Lanes. Before class, they smoked high-quality weed, and depending on whom you talked to, the marijuana either helped or hindered their scores. Birdie found it raised his average from 140 to 160 by the end of the quarter. They would need to "borrow" the balls from the bowling alley because, as Birdie noted, "Once you find a good ball, you want to hang on to it."

Birdie then received a letter from his buddy Frank Silas from Oklahoma, who worked for the National Park Service and lived in the infamous Cabin 52. If read:

Dear Birdie,
We sure had quite a summer. Hope you're settled in back at school. I'm at the University of Oklahoma studying to be a physical therapist. It's a pretty intense program, so I'll be here for a few more years. I will return to Crater Lake next summer. I sure love Oregon. You asked me about how I got a job with the Park Service. Actually, I was a congressional appointee. I went through my congressman, who helped facilitate my hire at Crater Lake. I would suggest you contact one of your senators from Oregon and see if they can help. Keep me posted on how it goes.

Take care, buddy,
Okie Frank

His encouragement was all the motivation Birdie needed. Now that he had experienced a summer in the Cascades, he anticipated the prospect of a summer job with the Park Service or Forest Service to help fund his college education. He initiated his correspondence with Senator Mark Hatfield and Senator Bob Packwood. In both letters, he inquired about the possibility of a congressional appointment to work outdoors for the federal government.

Incredibly, Birdie heard back in less than two weeks from Senator Packwood.

Dear Mr. McInnes:
Thank you for your recent letter regarding your interest obtaining summer employment with the federal government. I believe you are following the proper procedure by taking the Civil Service Commission summer employment examination. If you should do well in the examination, I am certain that you will be able to find a position with the federal government. If you would send me the results of your examination, I would be very happy to contact the Forest Service or the National Park Service on your behalf.

Best wishes,
Bob Packwood

Birdie considered the official missive a good omen: he might have an opportunity for a federal job for the following summer. He did not want to suffer through another summer in Portland after experiencing Crater Lake. Shortly after hearing from Senator Packwood, Birdie took the test and squeaked by with a passing grade.

He then received a letter sent by the United States Civil Service Commission.

Dear Mr. McInnes:
On the basis of the information you furnished and the results of the written examination, you are eligible for hire.

Birdie was off on the right foot. His future looked bright.

Anticipating Halloween parties on the horizon during his last months in Portland, Birdie and Vin Beasley rented elaborate costumes at Helen's Costumer in downtown Portland. Both spent more money than they could afford, but the costumes were outrageous. Vin selected a gorilla suit, and Birdie chose a bear costume. They rented the gear for the entire weekend and made full use of their investment, starting with a party with their friends. Making their grand entrance, they were met with howls of laughter. Afterward, Vin and Birdie visited some of the cooler bars in downtown Portland, where they again were well received, especially with the ladies. Birdie acquired a few of their phone numbers, but those were long gone by morning.

Unfortunately for Vin, he was unable to remove his costume when he returned home except for the head, because the zipper in the back jammed. Tired and wasted, he slept in the costume the whole night. By morning, he was dripping wet as if he had slept in a sauna. He required Birdie's help with the zipper to escape the soggy suit.

In November, Birdie received a letter from the Forest Service. It read:

> Dear Mr. McInnes:
> This is an offer of employment—an opportunity to spend the summer out-of-doors, helping with the protection and management of national forest land. We have the application you signed and a copy of the letter to you from our Washington office.
>
> The position for which you are being considered is described on the enclosed sheet. Your acceptance or declination should be sent to the following address immediately: Forest Supervisor, Malheur National

Forest, 139 Dayton Street, John Day, Oregon 97845. Crews are now being organized, and we must hear from you promptly. This is a popular region with many outstanding attractions. We hope you will join us.

With a job in the bag for the summer of '74, Birdie was relieved. The next step was to begin preparations for his move to Eugene, which would require a couple of reconnaissance trips. Lu' was also interested in attending UO, so they drove to Eugene on a scouting mission and to stop by a party at Chaz Reece's house in Springfield, and they looked forward to another rite of passage: attending a UO football game.

Downtown Eugene, Oregon, and Spencer Butte

Chaz promised the boys there would be lots of females, but when they arrived, only three other people were present: Chaz's brother-in-law, his sister, and a friend. Evaluating the situation, Birdie and Lu' said farewell after a quick beer. On the way to the Duck game, they stopped at the College Side Inn near Lane Community College before attending the football game in Autzen Stadium. The Fighting Ducks played the Arizona State Sun Devils that night.

At the College Side Inn, it was "dimers night," meaning ten short beers for a dollar. "What a deal," exclaimed Birdie.

As they selected a table in the loft, they spotted about twenty hits of speed. "What luck!" said Lu'. "We can party all night."

After downing two dozen four-ounce beers, they were primed for a football game.

The Ducks weren't very good that year, but no matter. It was a college football game. Meeting other friends from Portland, they all sat together in the student section. Soon the Ducks were losing, and some students were growing increasingly inebriated and ill mannered. Some lost control and were removed by security. After the game, Birdie and Lu' still had energy, so they drove back to Portland.

Unfortunately, Birdie had accomplished nothing in terms of finding a living arrangement. He started planning his next trip. In December, he ventured to Eugene again. He scoured the Eugene-Springfield area, looking for an apartment close to campus, but the only one available was a "budget" basement apartment in "felony flats," a low-rent district in the Whiteaker neighborhood, which was sketchy, but it would have to do. Birdie had seen much worse in Portland. After all, he had lived in a place deemed Foul House.

Back in town for one last fling, Birdie celebrated his twenty-first birthday with his friends at Jack 'n' Jill's, a bar near Mt. Hood Community College. Coincidentally, the musical act happened to feature Elvin Bishop, whom he had recently seen at the Jackson County Fairgrounds. As Birdie celebrated his birthday, he couldn't help but observe his friends and conclude that escaping the City of Roses would be for the best. Many of his mates appeared mired in Portland, resigned to their fate.

Two weeks later, packed and ready to move, Birdie bade farewell to his family; his mom seemed anxious, and he had reconciled with his dad. Both parents were happy he would be continuing his college education. His siblings would miss him but knew he would be back on weekends for laundry duties and visits with friends. Wistful as he departed, Birdie feared that if he didn't leave now, he might never leave, which frightened him. Portland was delightful, a great place to grow up, but leaving would be an inevitable consequence of finding himself. In the end, he abandoned his beloved hometown and never returned as a resident.

Birdie now realized what Thomas Wolfe meant in *You Can't Go Home Again*. He reflected on the notion that his life had changed over the course of the summer, and consequently, he would never be the same. Portland, Birdie's hometown, would never feel the same either. Life was a paradox, and Birdie learned his path in life could be accomplished only by his own reckoning, for better or worse.

www.ingramcontent.com/pod-product-compliance
Lightning Source LLC
LaVergne TN
LVHW011714060526
838200LV00051B/2901